Scottish Country Kitchen

RUTH SHANNON

PHOTOGRAPHY BY GRAEME WALLACE

Publishing

Design – Melvin Creative
Printing – Toppan, China

Published by
GW Publishing
Box 15070
Dunblane,
FK15 5AN.

Tel +44 (0)1786 823278
www.gwpublishing.com

ISBN 978-0-9570844-1-4

I dedicate this book to my great aunt Alison Ballantyne

BLAIR CASTLE IN PERTHSHIRE

Scottish
Country
Kitchen

Contents

{7}

FENTON TOWER IN NORTH BERWICK

{8}

Foreword

Simplicity is the key to the best food dishes. I don't like to over-complicate my recipes. I believe that it is important to enjoy the distinctive natural flavours that we are so fortunate to have at our disposal.

But although we are nowadays far more health conscious than we used to be about the way we eat, we are also becoming more adventurous.

That said, I always insist on cooking with ingredients that are in season and locally sourced. I use pheasants in the winter; raspberries in the summer, and asparagus in June and July. All of my recipes have been created with ingredients that are readily available so that one doesn't have to travel miles to find them.

There is nothing more delicious than fresh fish, and especially shellfish. We have great salmon rivers in Scotland and there is a plentiful supply of lobster, crab and scallops to be found in our coastal waters.

In addition, we are especially lucky to have locally reared beef cattle and lamb that has been well hung, and we have a reputation for nurturing the best venison in the world. With an abundance of fruit berries and home grown vegetables, Scotland rewards us with a truly diverse range of produce to both cherish and enjoy.

The recipes in my book are largely based on well known British and international dishes using Scottish flavours.

You can't get better than that.

Ruth Shannon

Ruth Shannon

Introduction by Roddy Martine

To the south-west of Edinburgh, on the main street of the small dormitory village of Juniper Green, sits an unexpected find: a modest yet vibrant pavement tea room called Ruth's Kitchen.

You first notice it when your eye is caught by the wicker baskets of cascading flowers hanging on its exterior. Through the windows there are colourful displays of cakes and home baking. Pretty tablecloths overlay table tops adorned with fine china and simple, elegant cutlery.

These are the features that initially catch the attention of the passers-by drawing them inside. There is a welcoming, timeless charm about such places; an aura of good taste, courtesy and order, qualities both espoused and summed up by the proprietress of Ruth's Kitchen, Ruth Shannon herself.

Cookery in all of its varied forms, tastes and superlative techniques has been Ruth Shannon's life. Her paternal Ballantyne ancestors were from the Scottish Borders, and although she herself was Yorkshire- born, at Keighley, in England, her childhood was profoundly influenced by her father's Scottish family who in 1965 re-located from the small Peeblesshire village of Walkerburn to the east coast seaside town of North Berwick.

It was here at North Berwick, under the supervision of Great Aunt Alison, that Ruth first learned how to make scones when she was no more than twelve years old.

"Great Aunt Alison was a great old fashioned cook who had trained at the Edinburgh School of Cookery in Atholl Crescent, and could turn her hand to anything," Ruth recalls affectionately. "She liked nothing better than to entertain her friends and family with delicious lunches and dinners."

For Ruth, she was inspirational, telling her loads of stories about how she had catered for the military during the Second World War and afterwards worked in various Abbeyfield Homes. She was a great character and was very much admired by everybody who knew her.

Great Aunt Alison's influence in Ruth's childhood was therefore profound, and when her sister, Ruth's grandmother, became unwell, Ruth moved up from Yorkshire to live in North Berwick and look after her. At the same time, this enabled her to sign up for a Cordon Bleu cookery course at Edinburgh's Telford College.

In order to attend classes, Ruth rented a flat in Edinburgh for two years, and travelled back and forth to North Berwick at weekends. She was now on track, and on completing her training began her first paid employment at the Cramond Inn, a picturesque riverside pub on the outskirts of the Scottish Capital. It was here that she met up with a lady called Diana Russell, who at the time helped out in making the desserts.

"Diana and her husband owned The Luggie Restaurant in Pitlochry," Ruth explains. "When they later started up a franchise at the Murrayfield Golf Club, they asked me if I would be interested in helping them cater for functions. I agreed and, as a result, I soon learned a tremendous amount about the practical side of the catering business, very much more hands-on than the stuff I'd been taught at college. It also helped me to become a lot more self-confident."

And, indeed, it led to her travelling south into England to take on the catering responsibilities at Ockley Golf Club, near Dorking, before moving on to Huddersfield, where she worked in an Italian restaurant, taking time off to spend two seasons in Greece cooking at a taverna on the romantic island of Corfu.

The Italian restaurant and the taverna in Corfu were the start of Ruth's fascination with international cuisine. "The Greek episode in

particular made me realise that there were all kinds of different ways to prepare food," she says. "You just need to be inventive and be prepared to try out things you haven't done before. I found it all very exciting."

Returning home, Ruth was offered a position at Deene Park, near Corby in Northamptonshire, the historic home of the Brudenell family. The house and gardens were open to the public during the summer months and not only was Ruth responsible for supplying Deene Park's shop and 'Old Kitchen' tea room with a selection of home made cakes and scones, she also catered for private and corporate shooting and house parties.

"A number of the guests who came to stay there used to ask me if I'd be interested in cooking for fishing lodges in Scotland, and this got me thinking," she says. "I liked the idea of travelling around the country and being more independent, so I decided to get in touch with Annie Fraser who runs the Lovat Cooking Agency.

"Annie sent me off on my first booking to Syre Lodge on the River Naver in Sutherland. It was a bit of a challenge at first, going to work on my own in an entirely unknown environment, in a strange kitchen and in a relatively cut-off location, but I soon started to enjoy myself enormously. I loved the mix of people I met, and they obviously liked what I did for them as they started not only to re-book me, but to tell their friends about me."

For Ruth, it was the beginning of an immensely satisfying series of adventures, catering for country house parties the length and breadth of the north and south of Scotland – at Bettyhill in Sutherland; the Orton estate on the River Spey; Gruinard, on the River Carron; the Strathconon estate near Muir of Orde; Chesthill in Glen Lyon, Perthshire; Park House at Drumoak

in Kincardineshire; Kincardine Castle at Kincardine O'Neil, and Manderston House at Duns, in Berwickshire.

With further bookings at Jura House; Monteviot House at Jedburgh; Kindrochet Lodge on the Blair Atholl estate, and Fenton Tower in East Lothian, Ruth's CV starts to look as if it is a Who's Who of Scotland's greatest sporting destinations.

No wonder she was popular. For stalking parties, she prepared her very own apple fruitcake; for shooting lunches she provided venison stew made with leeks, and a game pie accompanied by fruit and local cheeses. "When I cooked at Jura House, I used to have to prepare the food in advance and take all of it over with me on the ferry," she recalls with some amusement. "More often than not, the game was shot by the house guests, but even when their requirements were pretty straightforward, I always tried to make my menus just that little bit more interesting."

It therefore comes as no surprise to learn that it was in the course of this annual circuit of Scotland's finest sporting estates that Ruth was able to collate her store of recipes, drawing upon an ever broadening expertise on how and where to source her food locally. Through being obliged to acquire her basic ingredients in some of the remotest, often almost inaccessible corners of the countryside, she rapidly realised just what a treasure chest was on offer.

For Scotland has it all, from the fresh lobsters, oysters, prawns, mussels, crab, scallops and white fish of the Atlantic and North Sea coastlines, the venison and feathered game from the hills and forests, the exceptional quality beef and lamb of the farmlands, the salmon and trout from the rivers and inland lochs, to the potatoes, mushrooms, carrots, asparagus, turnips,

cauliflowers, cabbages and leeks, and strawberries, raspberries, apples, pears, plums and blackberries of the hinterland.

Although traditionally a poor country by historic repute, Scotland's indisputable wealth has always been in its rain-washed rural landscape and the richness of its seasonal environment, a reality that is so often forgotten in an age which at its peril chooses to turn its back on the land that feeds it. In an increasingly urban and populous society, there are few of us who realise just how immensely fortunate we are in having such valuable renewable resources so readily available on our doorstep.

And not just on the land.

From coast to coast, in the estuaries of the east and west mainland, and off-shore from the Inner and Outer Hebrides, and the far flung islands of Orkney and Shetland, there exists an immensely rich and varied harvest of seafood. Fisheries employed in the processing of Herring, Atlantic Cod and Sprat, are a staple industry of the Hebridean and north-west of Scotland economy. Scotland's off-shore sea fishing fleet currently employs in the region of 5,205 fishermen, and operates in the region of 2,224 coastal vessels, which are nowadays largely taken up with the gathering of shellfish (Langoustine, Brown Crab, Scallops, Squid and Lobster) using creels, trawls and dredges. A substantial percentage of this catch is exported, but it is nonetheless readily available locally for those who want it.

Shallow, sheltered water, with the tidal streams of the Pentland Firth, provides the ideal breeding ground for Velvet Crab, Lobster and Brown Crab. Orkney, with its archipelago of little islands embracing 1,000 miles of coastline, has the largest Brown Crab fishery in the UK, landing 2000 tonnes of crab meat every year, over twenty per cent of the total Scottish catch.

The fishing industry of the Western Isles has also largely diversified into procuring shellfish, notably for the Spanish market. The main centres of activity are on the island of Scalpay (Prawns and Scallops), at Loch Roag on the west coast of Lewis (Lobster, Crab and Dogfish), Stornoway, the Capital of Lewis (Prawns and Crab), Berneray, on North Uist (Lobster and Velvet Crab), Grimsay, south east of Benbecula (Prawns and Velvet Crab), on the Isle of Eriskay (Crab and Lobster) and on Barra (Prawns and Scallops).

Despite a steadily growing home demand, the greater proportion of this rich sea harvest is despatched by ship to mainland Europe: Langoustine to France, Spain and Italy; Crab to France, Spain and Portugal; Shell Scallops to Spain, France and Italy, and Squid to Spain. The appetite of mainland Europe for shellfish is insatiable.

However, because of the nature of its preparation, Lobster tends to be almost exclusively retained for the domestic market. On a personal note, I have to confess that the most succulent lobster that I have ever tasted in my life was caught on the very same day in the waters around the Outer Hebridean island of Lewis.

Meanwhile, Scotland's white fish fleets continue to operate from ports in the North East such as Peterhead, Fraserburgh and Macduff, mostly preoccupied with catching Haddock, Cod and Saithe (Coley). The processing of the fish thereafter largely takes place in the Grampian Region before being widely dispersed to independent fishmongers and supermarkets throughout the UK home market. Once this market has been satisfied, the principal demand for Herring and Mackerel comes from the Netherlands, Germany and Russia.

In the context of uncertainties over Global

Warming and the European Union's strictures on fish quotas, it is doubly reassuring to learn that there are a number of highly pro-active UK Government-supported bodies in place to guarantee the future sustainability of Scotland's sea fishing industry and to secure the supply of healthy, safe, and high quality fish to the consumer.

Ruth's Luxury Fish Pie, as one might expect, is a succulent compilation of the very best, incorporating as it does Haddock, Cod, Scallops, and Peeled Prawns mixed in with Hard Boiled Eggs, chopped up with Parsley, Button Mushrooms and Maris Piper Potatoes. Another of her speciality dishes is Halibut with Cherry Tomatoes and Thyme. Her recipe for Sea Bass with Garlic, Lime and Herbs is equally agreeable.

Similar quality control guidelines to those governing fish are in position in the UK relating to the provenance of red meat produce. All of us have the right to know where the food on our plates originates, and nowhere is this more understood than in asserting the outstanding quality of Scotland's beef and lamb produce. Breeds of cattle such as Galloway, Aberdeen Angus, Shorthorn and Highland raised in lush pastures are certain to produce a better quality and tastier meat as a direct result of the high levels of natural vitamins and minerals inherent in the land that they occupy.

Black or red coated, with the characteristic white belt encircling their bodies, Galloways, as the name implies, are a hardy breed found on the exposed uplands of Galloway, in the South West of Scotland. Easily managed, Aberdeen-Angus is the fastest growing breed of beef cattle in the British Isles and now widely dispersed throughout the world. The Beef Shorthorn is to be found listed in the oldest herd book in the world, dating from 1822, and despite some controversial cross-breeding with the Maine-Anjou breed from France; they still prevail throughout the UK.

Scotland's most famous breed of cattle, as typified in the foreground of many a dramatic Victorian landscape painting, is undoubtedly Highland. Existing on the vast, rain soaked acreages of bleak mountain scenery, these hardy beasts, with their straggling red hair and sweeping horns, thrive where no other cattle breed could possibly exist. It appears that the climate and the rough terrain suit them because pure Highland beef today commands a premium price over all other beef because of its fine lean texture, succulent flavour, and healthy eating appeal.

Similar principles to those governing the production and supply of beef to the general public are also associated with Scotland's quality lamb products, notably Scottish Blackface, which consist of the Perth type, found mainly in the east of Scotland, and the Lanark type, which is integrated with the Newton Stewart type and is thus the dominant breed.

Cheviots, having originated from the tough glens and coastal lands of Caithness are also popular for cross-breeding with other hill breeds, a common practice. The Scotch Mule, for example, is a cross between the Blue Faced Leicester ram and the Scottish Blackface dam. Texels, imported into Scotland from France in the 1970's, do well in the sparse vegetation of upland regions and excel on the better pastures of the Lowlands. producing hardy cross-bred lambs when mixed with Scottish Blackface, as well as other breeds. Finally, there are the Shetland sheep which, although now considered unique to the Shetland Isles, were originally introduced over a millennium ago from Norway to these far-flung outposts of Scotland's northernmost possessions.

Across all of these varieties, the meat is renowned for being exceptionally tender and versatile. Ruth exemplifies this endorsement with her roasting instructions, going on to show how to prepare Lamb Shanks with Roasted Root Vegetables, a Moroccan Lamb Tagine, and a fillet of Lamb with Redcurrant, Red Wine and Mint Sauce.

Although Ayrshire bacon remains world-renowned, the majority of Scotland's most productive pig farms are still to be found in the North East. In an affectionate reference to her childhood, Ruth provides detailed advice on how to roast Pork, accompanying this with advice on how to make a mouth-watering Apple Sauce and a delicious Sage and Onion Stuffing.

Chicken is probably not considered to be the most exotic dish for serious gourmets to enthuse over, but it nevertheless remains immensely popular in its various manifestations, and besides, the meat is almost always readily available. From Coq au Vin incorporating Onions, Celery and Cognac, a recipe which she admits to having acquired from a friend, Ruth goes on to create her magic with Chicken with Saffron and Roasted Cherry Tomatoes, Chicken Breasts wrapped in Parma Ham with griddled Asparagus, and Chicken Breasts with Lime and Honey.

The left-overs, as she affirms, can easily be transformed into a delicious stock, and by adding Ginger and Garlic, Cornflour, Lime Juice and Zest, Soy Sauce, Sherry and Red Wine Vinegar to it, she tells you how to make Stir-fried Chicken with Cashew Nuts. Absolutely delicious with noodles.

It was the Victorians who transformed the Scottish countryside into a seasonal sporting playground, with wealthy members of British society migrating annually to the famous stalking, shooting and fishing estates of the Lowlands, and Highlands and Islands. Queen Victoria started the trend when she refurbished Balmoral Castle on Royal Deeside, her family members and their descendants religiously setting off into the hills and onto the heather-clad moors with their shotguns and ghillies. Even the late Queen Elizabeth The Queen Mother was to be found every autumn up to her waist in waders and casting for salmon in the River Dee.

In a race to be fashionable and to keep up with the idiosyncrasies of High Society, ancient clan castles were renovated and great mansions built on the spoils of the Industrial Revolution. As a consequence, the pursuit of game and its attendant rituals rapidly became associated with the indulgences of the idle rich, but this is not entirely fair.

For centuries, the culling of Red Deer and the management of Red Grouse have been essential priorities in the survival of the species. The quotas for Deer Stalking and for Walked Up and Driven Grouse Shooting are therefore strictly monitored. Times have moved on since King George V shot a thousand pheasants in one day, but the popularity of recreational sporting opportunities has certainly not abated.

Nor has the appetite for Venison off the-hill, Pheasant, Woodcock and Wild Pigeon from the woodlands, Grouse from the heather coated moors, Duck from the lochs and lochans, and Partridge from the cultivated fields of the Lowlands.

The rituals surrounding game shooting and the stalking of wild deer are fiercely entrenched in the stones of tradition. Deer see bright colours and quick movement, so it is important that the rules are obeyed. Those stalking must be physically fit, but able to remain still when required and they must

always dress in clothes which blend in with the heather.

Those privileged enough to take part in this most challenging of blood sports must first prove their rifle or shotgun skills by accompanying the head stalker to a dummy target. Nobody should even consider participating unless they are first able to shoot a group of three shots within a 10cm target at 100m. Having proved their worth, however, they must thereafter acknowledge the expertise of the stalker or ghillie allocated to look after them.

"It is a serious business," confides one legendary Highland stalker of my acquaintance. "When people are put in your charge you must first ascertain if they can shoot and if they have been stalking before. Then you tell them they can take as long as they like or as short as they like, but they know that you'll be watching them.

"And once the trigger is pulled, that is when the work starts," he continued. "Folk often forget that when a stag has been shot, it still has to be gralloched and taken down the hill on the back of a pony to the estate larder to be skinned."

Nowadays, the majority of the larger Scottish estates lease out their sporting rights to syndicates, thus contributing substantial sums to the rural economy. Deer stalking (Red Deer and Roe) has therefore not only spawned a valuable financial lifeline for the economy of the Highlands and Islands, but it has elevated venison to the finest restaurant kitchens in the land. Recent statistics have shown that the demand is rapidly exceeding its availability, but at the same time it should also be emphasised that the supervision of the red deer population is being strictly monitored by Scottish National Heritage, which in 2010 merged with the Deer Commission for Scotland (DCS).

From her experience working on so many of the finest sporting estates, you would naturally expect Ruth's game dishes to excel and she does not disappoint. In the following pages, she shows you the best way to roast a Haunch of Roe Deer, how to prepare Devilled Pheasant, how to roast young Partridge with Smoked Bacon, and how to serve Duck Breasts with Rowan Jelly, Port and Orange Sauce (garnished with poached Kumquats).

The Salmon Fishing Season, that other great sporting pastime, officially begins on the River Tay in January, followed up on the River Dee, River Spey and River Tweed in February. The Brown Trout season starts in March, although there is no closed season for Rainbow Trout, which is not an indigenous species to the UK and can be fished all the year round.

Salmon and trout continue to be enormously popular luxury fish dishes, and Ruth's Poached Salmon with Cucumber and Dill Sauce, her Salmon Fillets with Honey, Soy Sauce and Ginger, and her Trout with Toasted Almonds prove that the simplest recipes combined with a bit of creativity can achieve a triumph of texture and flavour.

Of course, a significant result of the abundance of seasonal salmon and trout, not to mention venison, is that, following on the popularity of such traditional delicacies as Loch Fyne Kippers, Finnan Haddies, and Arbroath Smokies, a major smoked produce industry has evolved to meet an escalating international demand. While Ruth's first course favourites in this book include Smoked Salmon Roulade and Smoked Trout Paté, she additionally provides expert instruction on how to prepare your very own and absolutely delicious Gravadlax.

In the eighteenth century, it was derisively claimed by the English lexicographer Dr

Samuel Johnson that oats were the staple diet of the Scottish nation. The fact is that Scots have always been immensely practical in making the best of what they have in abundance, and oats, aside from being easily cultivated in a damp climate, are readily adaptable as the component parts of such universally applauded Scottish clichés as haggis, porridge, and Scotch grain whisky. As Ruth insists, it is all about using basic ingredients and using your imagination.

And that wisdom especially applies to that other ubiquitous component of the culinary arts, the humble, or not so humble, potato. Cultivated on more than 3,700 holdings, Scottish producers currently grow over a million tonnes annually. The majority of crops are ranged along the east coast, from the Moray Firth and south into the Borders. The average consumer is probably unaware of this, but there are in the region of 450 different varieties of potato cultivated throughout the UK, with around 80 species being cultivated commercially.

The softer-skinned Rocket or Maris Bard are planted in the winter, ready for harvesting in the spring or early summer and generally referred to as 'new potatoes'. The firmer skinned, described as "maincrop" potatoes, are harvested in late summer or early autumn, and sold in supermarkets from September to May.

For roasting, Ruth prefers Maris Piper or King Edward, but she also provides instructions on how to roast New Potatoes with Rosemary and Garlic, and how to prepare a dish of Dauphinoise Potatoes with Grated Garlic, Ground Black Pepper and Parmesan Cheese.

From her experiences working in the Italian restaurant in Huddersfield, Ruth momentarily diversifies into creating a delicious Gnocchi with Spinach and Goat's Cheese. To cater for vegetarian tastes, she shows you how to prepare Asparagus and Camembert Tart, and Tomato, Leek and Cheese Puff.

A mild, rainy climate, predominantly cool in summer, delivers a natural advantage to the growing of Peas and Beans, Swedes, Carrots and Calabrese (a pre-winter form of Broccoli). Generally speaking, Beetroot, Broccoli, Brussel Sprouts, Cabbage, Carrots, Chicory, Leeks, Mushrooms, Parsnips, Potatoes, Turnips, Kale, Squash, Shallots, Celeriac, and Celery are readily available from January; Asparagus and Spinach from May; Broad Beans and Broccoli from June; Runner Beans, Courgettes and Shallots in July; Pumpkins in October, and Parsnips, Red Cabbage and Leeks in November and December.

Those same climatic conditions apply to fruit, which although naturally dependant upon the seasons, is equally abundant throughout Scotland.

The primary berry growing territories are to be found in Tayside, notably in the sheltered Strathearn/ Strathmore valleys. Grampian Region, the Highlands, the Isle of Arran, Ayrshire and the Border country are equally fertile areas for fruit farming. Berries thrive in the cool summers where long daylight hours allow them to ripen with a wonderful richness of flavour. Over 2,400 tonnes of raspberries and 4,600 tonnes of strawberries are grown in Scotland every year.

In season between July and September, Blueberries (otherwise know as Blaeberries), have recently soared in popularity, as have Blackberries (Brambles), which thrive in abundance in the wild. Something to remember is that the majority of fruit farms, notably around Blairgowrie and in the Glens of Angus, encourage customers to come in person to pick their own requirements.

Another phenomenon of the twentieth and

twenty first centuries has been a spectacular revival in the creation of traditional home-made farmhouse cheeses, several inspired by the soft and flavourful variations made in Europe and elsewhere. There are now more than two dozen independent local cheese-makers to be found across Scotland, ranging from industrial cheddar creameries to much smaller-scale soft cheese producers. Therefore, to round off her collection of recipes, Ruth has supplied us with a superb list, singling out some of her favourites.

As she informs us, there is nothing more satisfying or rewarding than rounding off a perfect dinner with a mixed cheese platter accompanied by some crisp crackers and a fruity port, or, dare I suggest, a single malt Scotch Whisky.

Throughout her immensely enterprising career, Ruth Shannon has acquired an instinctive talent for sourcing her ingredients locally. Her skills have therefore never been curtailed by the lack of available ingredients, but she says that you must always bear in mind that Scotland's distinctly defined seasons of Winter, Spring, Autumn and Summer play a critical role in the availability of produce – pheasant in the Autumn and Winter; raspberries in Summer.

This taken into account, Ruth insists that her vegetables have always to be

fresh from the market place and compatible with what she is serving. "Lovely red cabbage is a perfect accompaniment for venison, or griddled asparagus in June, July and October, "she says. "The thing with venison is that there is no fat, so it goes perfectly with little wild mushrooms." Absolutely yummy.

Talking us through the recipes in this book, Ruth clearly enthuses over the delights of creating Smoked Haddock Soufflés, Tomato and Thyme Tartlets, and game dishes such as Fillet of Venison with a Port Sauce and Shitake Mushrooms. Her Game Pie (Diced Venison with Pheasant and Partridge Breasts) is another speciality. "I can make anything with the right ingredients," she insists shyly, singling out her Moroccan Lamb Tagline, with its Apricots, Saffron, Spices and Lemon, as an unexpected example.

As a first course, she particularly likes to serve Dill and Salmon Filo Parcels, Gravadlax, or a Smoked Trout and Pink Grapefruit Salad.

Her favourites for the main course include Beef Wellington, made with Aberdeen Angus, and Sticky Pork Spare Ribs. Some of my own favourite recipes in the following pages include Pheasant Breasts with Fennel, Roast Partridge, Pigeon with Rowan Jelly, Port and Orange Sauce, and a mouth-watering Duck with Black Cherries

"People always seem to be very nervous about preparing lobster," she observes, going on to say that she herself prefers to serve lobster cold with a Chive and Lemon Mayonnaise. How could anyone find fault with that?

"I know that vegetarian dishes are not a particularly Scottish thing to do, but so many people nowadays have become vegetarians that you absolutely have to consider them," she continues. "Funnily enough, I find that my Gnocchi with Spinach and Goats Cheese and Asparagus and Camembert Tarts are just as popular with non-vegetarians."

Ruth thinks that really simple food is always best, but she is not that keen on nursery type puddings. "I know that there are some people who love them, but it can all become a bit stodgy if you are not careful."

On the other hand, she adores home made ice cream. "An absolute winner is my Ginger and Chocolate Ice Cream," she says. "With just a bit of variation, you can do absolutely amazing things using berries, particularly fresh raspberries and gooseberries."

The world of the creative cook is full of surprises, whether making new discoveries, perfecting variations on an old favourite or coming up with something entirely new and original.

Ruth's Halibut with Cherry Tomatoes and Thyme, for example, is just as much of a triumph as her White Chocolate Mousse with Nectarine and Raspberry Coulis and her Passion Fruit Soufflés. "It is all about having that extra courage to do something just that little bit different," she claims.

Despite her immense enjoyment of cooking for the sporting lodge and country house circuit, Ruth was becoming tired of constantly having to travel from place to place, and only being able to return home for brief respites. Realising that it was perhaps time for a change, she therefore began to look around for something a bit different, an occupation that would enable her to become marginally more settled in the life she had chosen.

The opportunity arose in 2010 when she saw a newspaper advertisement for an old fashioned tea room for sale on the outskirts of Edinburgh.

Later in that same year, Ruth's Kitchen was launched.

{22}

Soups

Chicken Stock

Vegetable Stock

Cream of Celery Soup

Vegetable and Butter Bean Soup

Exotic Mushroom Soup

Game Soup

Tomato and Basil Soup

Pea and Mint Soup

Scallop Chowder{23}

Using a Magimix

For most smooth soups, sauces and Hollandaise I like to use the Magimix which is also very good for grating and slicing with its separate attachments.

If you do not have a Magimix you could use an ordinary blender to achieve a similar result.

Chicken Stock

Ingredients
8 Chicken wings or thighs
2 Onions halved with skin on
2 Carrots halved
3 pints of water
A handful of Black Peppercorns

The basis to all good soups is a well made, old-fashioned chicken or vegetable stock.

Method

- Cover the chicken and vegetables with water and bring to the boil.
- Boil rapidly for 45 minutes.
- Simmer for a further 20 minutes.
- Strain the liquid through a strainer into another pan and keep warm.

Vegetable Stock

Ingredients
2 Onions halved with skin on
2 Carrots halved
4 Leeks cut into chunks
1 Celery head cut into chunks
3 Pints of water
A handful of Black Peppercorns

Method

- Same as above
- Alternatively if you don't have time to make stock from scratch you could use stock cubes, although the flavour of home made stock really gives a better soup.

Cream of Celery Soup Serves 6-8

Ingredients
75g/ 3oz Butter – slightly salted
1 tbsp Plain Flour
2 Heads of Celery – finely chopped
2 Onions – finely chopped
2 Carrots – finely chopped
2 pts Chicken Stock

Method

- You will need a large heavy-based pan.
- Melt the butter over a low heat.
- When melted add the chopped onions.
- Cook until soft then add the carrots and celery.
- Continue cooking over a low heat until the vegetables are soft.
- Stir flour in vigorously.
- Add stock a little at a time until the consistency is smooth.
- Keep stirring until all the liquid is incorporated.
- Season well with salt and pepper.
- Add more stock if you prefer slightly thinner soup.
- Blend in a Magimix until smooth.

{25}

Vegetable and Butter Bean Soup

Ingredients
2 pints Vegetable Stock
2 x 15oz Tins of Butter Beans
5 tbsp Olive Oil
2 Leeks – sliced thinly
2 Carrots – diced
2 Parsnips – diced
2 Onions – finely chopped
225g/ 8oz Back Unsmoked Bacon – cut into small dices
1 Head Celery – thinly sliced
Fresh Thyme and Parsley
1 Clove Garlic – finely chopped

This is lovely rustic soup, which I like to make a couple of days before needed as it improves in flavour.

Method

- Puree 1 tin of butter beans before you begin to prepare the soup and put to one side.
- Heat the oil in a large pan and add the diced bacon, onions, carrots, parsnips, leeks, garlic and celery.
- Cook evenly until the vegetables are soft then add the vegetable stock.
- Cook for 30 minutes.
- Then add the pureed beans to create a lovely thickness to the soup.
- Cook for a further 30 minutes.
- Finally add the whole butter beans, thyme and parsley.
- Taste then add salt and pepper as needed.

Exotic Mushroom Soup Serves 6

Ingredients

2 pts Chicken Stock

900g/ 2lbs Mushrooms – washed and sliced (You can use a mixture of chestnut, oyster, shiitake, flat and button)

60ml/ 2fl oz Sherry

60ml/ 2fl oz Single Cream

2 Onions

75g/ 2oz Butter

1 tbsp Plain Flour

Pinch of Ground Nutmeg

Pinch of Ground Black Pepper and Salt

I like to eat this soup without it being blended as it has a wonderful rustic taste. It is especially good with a slice of toasted French bread.

Method

⬜ Melt the butter then cook the onions until soft.

⬜ Add the mushroom and cook until soft.

⬜ Then add the plain flour and cook on a low heat until well incorporated.

⬜ Add the stock and stir well.

⬜ Add the sherry and cream and ground nutmeg.

⬜ Season with salt and pepper.

Game Soup

You will need a good game stock for this heart-warming winter soup.

Ingredients
2 Pheasant and 4 Partridge Carcasses
1 Large Onion – peeled and chopped
2 Sticks of Celery and 2 Carrots – chopped
2 Leeks – sliced
½ Swede – diced
6-8 Whole Peppercorns
2 Bay Leaves and 1 Generous Bunch of Parsley
1 Small Glass of Port
Juice of 1 Lemon
Salt and Pepper

Method

- Place all the ingredients in a large saucepan with a tight fitting lid and bring slowly to the boil.
- Simmer very gently for 3-3½ hours.
- Skim and drain the stock. Remove the meat from the carcass and shred into small pieces.
- Return the meat back to the strained stock.
- The vegetables should then be put into a Magimix or blender and pureed.
- Put the pureed vegetables into a large sieve over a bowl and press through until the puree is lovely and smooth.
- Return the pureed vegetables back into the game stock.
- Add a dash of port, lemon juice and salt and pepper to taste.

To Make Croutons

- Take 1 large Ciabatta Loaf and 1 tbsp of Olive Oil.
- Roughly cut the Ciabatta into chunky squares.
- Place in a roasting tin with a drop of olive oil and cook until crispy.
- Don't use too much olive oil as this makes the croutons too greasy.

You could make this two days before requiring it, as this really improves the quality. I like to serve this soup with rustic croutons.

Tomato and Basil Soup

Ingredients

1 tbsp Plain Flour
100g/ 2oz Butter
1 Carrot – diced
1 tsp Castor Sugar
1 tsp Oregano
1 Handful of Basil
2 Onions – finely chopped
450ml/ 15fl oz Tinned Tomatoes
500g/ 1 lb Cherry Tomatoes

This is delicious soup that looks as good as it tastes. Serve with fresh crusty bread to complement the wonderful tomato flavour and texture.

Method

▨ Melt the butter then add the onions and cook until soft.

▨ Add the carrots and cook until soft.

▨ Add the cherry tomatoes and cook for 5 minutes, then add tin of tomatoes.

▨ When incorporated well, add the plain flour and cook for a few minutes over a low heat.

▨ Then add the chicken stock and mix well.

▨ Add the castor sugar, basil and oregano.

▨ Cook for 20 minutes.

▨ Season with salt and pepper.

▨ Blend in Magimix, then strain into another pan for a lovely smooth soup.

Pea and Mint Soup

Ingredients

2 pints Chicken Stock

2 Large Potatoes – peeled and cut into large chunks

1 lb Frozen Petis Pois

1 tsp Castor Sugar

45g/ 1½ oz Butter

Good handful of Fresh Mint

2fl oz Single Cream

1 Onion – finely chopped

Ground Black Pepper

Method

- Melt the butter and add the finely chopped onion.
- Cook until soft then add the peas and mint.
- Cook for 5 minutes then add the potatoes followed by the chicken stock.
- Simmer until the potatoes are soft.
- Blend in a Magimix and transfer back to pan.
- Add the castor sugar and single cream.
- Finally, add ground black pepper to taste.
- Chill in the fridge for 3 to 4 hours.

{31}

This makes a delicious chilled summer soup when there is a plentiful supply of mint.

Scallop Chowder

This is a substantial soup, which can also serve as a light lunch with some crusty bread.

Ingredients

7 tbsp Virgin Olive Oil

15 Large Scallops with Roe on

2 Onions - skinned and finely sliced

2 Sticks of Celery – finely chopped

3 Carrots and 1 Orange Pepper – cut into fine Julienne sticks

4 Potatoes – peeled and cut into small dice

2 Saffron Strands

2 Vine Tomatoes – blanched, deseeded and cut into small dice

50g/ 2oz chopped Parsley

275ml/ ½ pt Double Cream

This is luxury soup, for special occasions. I usually allow 3 scallops per person.

For the Fish Stock

Boil up the following ingredients for 1 hour and then strain into a clean pan.

850ml/ 1½ pt Water

2 Onions – cut into quarters

Salmon Head and Bones from Shellfish or any Fish scraps

Method

- First prepare the fish stock as described above.
- Now, on a clean chopping board clean the scallops, taking off any membrane but leaving the roe intact.
- Rinse them in cold water, drain and put into a clean bowl.
- Heat half the olive oil in a large heavy-based pan and brown the scallops for just 1 minute on each side, as they will finish cooking in the soup.
- Transfer the scallops into another bowl and set aside.
- Heat the rest of the oil and add the onions. Cook for 2 minutes then add the celery, carrots, pepper and potatoes. Cook for 5 – 10 minutes.
- Keep stirring to mix evenly.
- Then add the fish stock, cream, lemon juice and saffron strands. Cook until the potatoes are cooked.
- Taste and add salt and pepper
- Just before serving add the strips of tomato and the scallops.
- Let the scallops heat in the soup for 3 –4 minutes so as not to overcook them.
- Garnish with the chopped parsley.

AN
EASY
LUNCH MENU

TOMATO AND BASIL SOUP

. . . .

COQ AU VIN

CREAMED POTATOES

FRENCH GREEN BEANS

GRATIN OF CAULIFLOWER

. . . .

LEMON MOUSSE WITH
ALMOND MACAROONS

This is a
really easy menu
as all the courses
can be prepared
in advance.

First Courses

Tomato and Thyme Tartlets

Twice Baked Gruyere Cheese Soufflés

Grilled Goats Cheese with Roasted Cherry Tomatoes and Pine Nuts

Tomato, Goats Cheese and Basil Tartlets

Roasted Peppers filled with Cherry Tomatoes, Garlic and Anchovies

Joy's Warm Asparagus, Pear and Parma Ham Salad

Figs, Goats Cheese and Parma Ham Salad

Avocado Mousse with Prawns

Smoked Salmon Roulade   {35}

Smoked Salmon and Dill Tartlets

Smoked Haddock Soufflés

Gravadlax

Griddled Scallops with a Lime Dressing

Fresh Salmon and Dill Filo Parcels with Hollandaise Sauce

Smoked Trout and Pink Grapefruit Salad

Smoked Trout Paté

Tomato and Thyme Tartlets

Ingredients
250g/ 9oz Puff Pastry – You can buy ready made puff pastry – Saxby's is the best
1 Large Onion – finely diced
2 tbsp Fresh Lemon Thyme
1 tsp Oregano
Salt and Pepper
2 Small Punnets Cherry Tomatoes
3 tbsp Olive Oil

For the Garnish
Basil Leaves
Stoned Black Olives
Olive Oil

Try eating them outdoors on a summer evening, with a chilled glass of Chablis. Delicious and very tasty, a real Mediterranean treat.

Method

- You will need 6 small individual tartlet tins or one 9" loose bottomed tartlet tin. Grease the tin/s well with the olive oil.
- Cut your pastry into six and then roll into thin rounds and fit into each tin. Alternatively if you want one large tartlet, roll the pastry and place in the 9" tartlet tin.
- Place in the fridge for half an hour.
- Melt the olive oil in a heavy-based pan on a medium heat and cook the onions until soft then add the thyme and oregano.
- Cut the cherry tomatoes in half vertically and put to one side.
- Remove the tartlet tins from the fridge and add the onion, thyme and oregano mixture.
- Then place the cherry tomatoes onto the onion, thyme and oregano mixture.
- Arrange the tomatoes so that the skins are sitting on the mixture and the flesh side is to the top.
- Brush the tomatoes lightly with olive oil.
- Place the tartlets on a baking tray in a hot oven – 225°C/ 450°F/ Gas 8.
- Cook for 25 –30 minutes until the pastry turns golden brown.
- Take the tartlets out of the oven 5 minutes before serving. This gives the tartlets time to rest, which makes it easier to lift them out of the tins.

To Serve
- To garnish, I put two basil leaves together with black olives sprinkled over the tartlet, with a drop of olive oil.

Twice Baked Gruyere Cheese Soufflés

Ingredients
450ml/ ¾ pt Milk
75g/ 3oz Butter
75g/ 3oz Plain Flour
Pinch of Dry English Mustard
Pinch of Ground Nutmeg
225g/ 9oz Gruyere Cheese – grated
6 Eggs – separated
425ml/ ¾ pt Single Cream or White Sauce

Method

- Firstly you will need to grease eight ramekin dishes.
- Preheat the oven to 230ºC/ 450ºF/ Gas 8.
- Melt the butter and stir in the flour and mustard.
- Add the milk then take off the heat continuing to whisk the mixture until smooth.
- Return to the heat and bring to the boil stirring all the time.
- Add 175g/ 7oz of the cheese and stir well.
- Add the egg yolks, salt and pepper and ground nutmeg.
- When the mixture is incorporated take off the heat.
- Whisk the egg whites until stiff and fold into the mixture.
- Stand the ramekin dishes in a roasting tin filled with boiling water.
- Divide the mixture between the eight ramekins.
- Cook for 15-20 minutes or until risen.
- Take out of the oven and leave soufflés until cool.
- Then turn them out onto a buttered ovenproof dish.
- Sprinkle the remaining Gruyere over the top of the soufflés and coat the edges of the soufflés with the cream or white sauce that has been seasoned.
- Bake for 15 minutes or until risen and brown.

Delicious!! Always a winner, especially when served with Stilton shortbread.

Stilton Shortbreads

I like to serve Stilton Shortbreads with the soufflés. I feel they really do gild the lily.

Ingredients
150g/ 6oz Plain Flour
1 tsp Salt
½ tsp Cayenne Pepper
75g/ 3oz Ground Fine Semolina
125g/ 5oz Crumbled Stilton
24g/ 1oz Stilton – for top of biscuits
150g/ 6oz Chilled Butter

I like to keep these wonderfully flavoured shortbreads warm to serve with the soufflés

Method
- Lightly butter a large baking tray and line with parchment.
- Mix together the flour, salt, cayenne pepper and semolina in a large bowl.
- Add the crumbled Stilton and butter and mix together until the consistency becomes dough like.
- Alternatively you can combine all the ingredients in the Magimix.
- Roll the pastry dough out on a floured surface to a ½" thickness.
- Cut with a 2" scone cutter and arrange on the baking sheet. Sprinkle a little Stilton on each shortbread.
- Bake at 150°C/ 300°F/ Gas 2 for 1 hour.

Grilled Goats Cheese with Roasted Cherry Tomatoes and Pinenuts

Serves 4

Ingredients

1 Small Punnet Yellow Santini Cherry Tomatoes

1 Small Punnet – Red Santini Cherry Tomatoes

4 Little Drums of Goats Cheese – this should be soft goats cheese

4 tbsp Olive Oil

175g/ 6oz Roasted Pine Nuts

Basil to Garnish

Method

- Preheat the oven to 230°C/ 450°F/ Gas 8.
- Cut each goats cheese drum in half to give 8 circles.
- Place the yellow and red cherry tomatoes into a small roasting tin with olive oil and cook until the tomatoes start to soften. Do not overcook.
- Place a small frying pan over a medium heat and cook the pinenuts stirring with a spoon until they turn golden.
- Turn the temperature down and mix the tomatoes and pinenuts together and keep warm in a low oven.
- Now turn on the grill and make sure it is hot.
- Cover the grill tray with foil and place the eight circles of goats' cheese an inch apart. Place the tray on the second shelf down so that the goats' cheese cooks evenly.
- Cook for 5-7 minutes only until the cheese is brown on top and runny in the middle.

To Serve

- To present this dish you will need four plates.
- Place two circles of goats' cheese in the middle of each plate then carefully spoon the tomato and pinenut mixture around the cheese. Decorate with basil leaves.

Enjoy!

Tomato, Goats Cheese and Basil Tartlets

Ingredients

Pastry
150g/ 6oz Sieved Plain Flour
75g/ 3oz Chilled Diced Butter
1½ tsp Freshly Grated Parmesan Cheese

Filling
Olive Oil
1 Large Red Onion – finely chopped
Fresh Basil
150g/ 6oz Soft Goats Cheese
1 Small Punnet Cherry Tomatoes
½ pt Single Cream
Freshly Ground Black Pepper

Method

- Firstly grease 6 tartlet cases.
- Combine pastry ingredients in a Magimix until the mixture resembles fine breadcrumbs.
- Divide the mixture and mould into the tartlet cases. Place in the fridge for one hour.
- Heat two tbsp of olive oil in a pan and add the red onion. Cook until soft and divide the onions between the tartlets.
- Cut the tomatoes in half adding 6 halves to each tartlet.
- Then add the goats' cheese which should be cut into large dices.
- Add three basil leaves to each tartlet.
- Mix the single cream and ground black pepper and pour over the tartlet cases.
- Cook in the oven at 180°C/ 350°F/ Gas 4 for 20 minutes or until set.

Roasted Peppers filled with Cherry Tomatoes, Garlic and Anchovies

Serves 6

Ingredients
4 Red or Yellow Peppers
4 Small Punnets Cherry Tomatoes cut in half
3 Cloves of Garlic – finely Chopped
1 Small Tin of Anchovies
Fresh Basil
1 tsp Oregano
1 Small Jar of Stones Black Olives
Olive Oil

Method
- Cut the peppers in half leaving the stalks on but discard the seeds.
- Place the cherry tomatoes into each halved pepper.
- Then add the finely chopped garlic and oregano.
- Cut each anchovy in half, length ways, and put two anchovy strips on each pepper, attractively arranging diagonally across each other.
- Add 1 tsp of olive oil to each pepper.
- Cook in a moderate oven 180°C/ 350°F/ Gas 4 for 25 minutes.

To Serve
- Decorate each pepper with a sprig of basil and three or four stoned black olives. Spoon over a trickling of olive oil to complete the dish.

{43}

This is a lovely healthy first course.

Joy's Warm Asparagus, Pear and Parma Ham Salad

I was given this recipe from a client who had an Australian cook catering for her one summer. It is one of those all time favourite warm salads that are so delicious when asparagus is in season. I just love it.

Ingredients
Salad leaves
18 Asparagus spears
2 Slices of Parma Ham
2 Ripe Pears - with skin intact
Olive oil

Method

- First trim the asparagus taking an inch off the stalks.
- Then cut the parma ham into small strips taking any fat off the edges.
- Cut the pears into six taking the core out but leaving the skins on.
- Now you will need to heat a large griddle pan with two tablespoons of olive oil.
- Add the asparagus in two batches onto the griddle pan turning frequently.
- Your asparagus will turn a lovely golden crispy colour.
- Put the asparagus in a Pyrex dish in a low oven to keep warm.
- Place the pears on the griddle pan until they become caramelised and soft, turning each pear 2-3 times.
- Add the pears to the asparagus.
- Put one tbsp of olive oil on the griddle pan and quickly fry the Parma ham for 1 -1½ minutes then mix the ham with the asparagus and the pears.

To Serve

- Place a few salad leaves on the centre of each plate
- Arrange the asparagus, pears and Parma ham attractively on the salad leaves.
- You will have some natural juices in the Pyrex dish which can be spooned over the individual salads for added flavour.

Figs, Goats Cheese and Parma Ham Salad

Ingredients
6 Whole Fresh Figs
12 Slices Parma Ham
200g/ 8oz Soft Ripe Goats Cheese
Olive Oil
2 tbsp Lemon Juice
Ground Black Pepper
1 Bag of Mixed Salad Leaves

Method

- Firstly halve the figs.
- Rip the goats' cheese into big pieces.
- Divide the lettuce leaves between the six plates.
- Arrange the salad by placing the figs on the Parma ham and then sprinkle on the goats cheese.
- Drizzle the lemon juice and olive oil over the salad with a touch of ground black pepper.

{47}

Avocado Mousse with Prawns

There are a lot of different variations of this recipe but I find this one to be light and refreshing. It also looks very pretty with the green avocado mixture against the pinkness of the prawns.

{48}

Ingredients
2 Ripe Avocados
Juice of ½ Lemon
5fl oz Vegetable Stock - hot
5fl oz Single Cream
5fl oz Hellmans Mayonnaise
1 sachet Gelatine
1 tsp Ground Black Pepper
8oz Medium sized cooked and peeled Prawns
55g/ 2oz chives – finely chopped
12 Cucumber Slices
1 Lemon cut into 6 slices
4 tbsps French Dressing

To Make the French Dressing
4fl oz Olive Oil
3 tbsp White Wine Vinegar
1 tsp Castor Sugar
5 Grinds of Black Pepper
Pinch of Salt
½ tsp English Mustard Powder

Method

- You will need to grease 6 dariole moulds or ramekin dishes with olive oil.
- First you must make the mousse.
- Stir the gelatine into the hot vegetable stock making sure that all the gelatine granules are dissolved.
- Put all the flesh of the avocados into the Magimix with the juice of ½ a lemon.
- Mix well then add the gelatine stock, blending to get a smooth mixture.
- With a spatula remove all the mixture and transfer it to a mixing bowl.
- Then add the single cream and mayonnaise, mixing well so there aren't any lumps from the mayonnaise.
- Add 1 tsp ground black pepper.
- Divide the mixture into your 6 moulds, cover with cling film, place on a small tray and put into the fridge for 2 hours or until set
- To make the French dressing mix all the ingredients so they are well combined.
- Place the prawns into a bowl and add the finely chopped chives.
- Add the French dressing and stir until evenly combined.

To Serve

- You will need 6 plates and with a warm table knife turn out your mousse onto the middle of each plate. Place 2 prawns on top of each mousse and drizzle the dressing round the plate.
- Garnish with the lemon and cucumber.

{49}

This is a lovely summer's evening first course. What could be nicer than sitting in the garden with this delicious starter and a crisp dry glass of Frascatti?

Smoked Salmon Roulade

I once saw this first course being prepared by a chef on a Mediterranean cruise line on the TV programme 'Wish You Were Here' many years ago. I have slightly adapted the recipe which has proven to be a very popular first course and so easy to assemble.

Use a good quality smoked salmon such as Summer Isles or Inverawe Smoked Salmon. I like to use my local fish supplier, Clarks Brothers at Fisherrow Harbour, Musselburgh, as they smoke their own salmon.

Ingredients

2 x 8oz (225g) Packs of Long Sliced Smoked Salmon
225g/ 8oz Cooked and Peeled Prawns
1 Spring Onions
1 x 250g/ 9oz Tubs of Philadelphia Cheese
Lea & Perrins Sauce
Tabasco

Method

- You will need 1 large sheet of greaseproof paper.
- First of all wash, top and tail the spring onions then finely slice.
- In a bowl, combine the Philadelphia cheese, prawns, spring onions, a dash of Lea & Perrins and Tabasco.
- Place the greaseproof paper on your worktop and carefully arrange the smoked salmon slices in layers.
- Next spread the mixture you have prepared over the salmon slices until the salmon is totally covered.
- Now roll the assembled smoked salmon as you would a swiss roll, to create the roulade.
- Place the roulade on to a large plate and put in the fridge for 3-4 hours until chilled.

To Serve

- Garnish your plates with lemon and cucumber.
- You will now need a large sharp knife dipped in hot water.
- Cut the roulade into 1" slices and allow 2 per person.

{51}

Smoked Salmon and Dill Tartlets

Ingredients

For the Pastry
6 oz/ 150g Sieved Plain Flour
3 oz/ 75g Chilled Diced Butter
1½ tsps freshly Grated Parmesan Cheese

For the Filling
225g/ 8oz Smoked Salmon – cut into small strips
2 Whole Eggs
Juice of ½ a Lemon
Fresh Dill
275ml/ ½ pint of Single Cream
Pinch of Ground Nutmeg and Mace

Method

{52}

- Place the pastry ingredients in the Magimix and mix until the pastry resembles fine breadcrumbs. Wrap in cling film and put into the fridge for one hour.
- Take the chilled pastry and mould into 6 tartlet cases.
- Bake at 180ºC/ 350ºF/ Gas 4 for 10-12 minutes.
- Take the tartlet cases out of the oven and leave to cool.
- Divide the smoked salmon between the tartlets and put the lemon juice over the smoked salmon.
- Now beat together the eggs, 1 tsp of dill and single cream with a grinding of black pepper, nutmeg and mace.
- Pour this mixture into the tartlets and leave for about 10-15 minutes or until set.
- Serve warm.

This is a delicious first course that can be prepared in advance, leaving you more time to enjoy being with your guests.

Smoked Haddock Soufflés

This is a delicious first course. So much so that one of the fishing lodges I cook at in the North West of Scotland, always makes a special request for me to make it. It is also so easy to prepare.

Ingredients
You will need 6 ramekin dishes – buttered
150g/ 6oz Smoked Haddock (un-dyed)
50g/ 2oz Butter
50g/ 2oz Plain Flour
1 pt Milk
2 Eggs – separated
Juice of ½ a Lemon
Salt and Pepper
Pinch of Ground Nutmeg

Method
- Cut the fish into large chunks and put into a pan with all the milk.
- Bring to the boil, then take off the heat and put to one side.
- In another pan melt the butter, add flour and mix well.
- Whisk in the milk that the haddock has been cooked in and mix until you have a smooth consistency.
- Add the egg yolks one at a time until all the mixture is combined evenly.
- Add smoked haddock, seasoning, lemon juice and nutmeg.
- Mix well until the fish has been incorporated.
- Leave the mixture to cool.
- Beat the egg whites till stiff then fold in to the fish mixture.
- Divide into the ramekin dishes and place them on a baking tray.
- Cook on 220°C /425°F/ Gas 7 – for 10-12 minutes.

Always make sure that your guests are sitting down first, as it is better for them to wait until it is prepared rather than the other way round.

Gravadlax

Gravadlax originates from Scandinavia. It has proved to be very popular in Scotland with the abundance of salmon in our great Scottish rivers.

Ingredients
A side of freshly caught Salmon
75g/ 3oz Fresh Dill
Coarse Rock Salt
Castor Sugar
2fl oz Whisky
The proportions of Rock Salt to Castor Sugar should be 38g/ 1½ oz salt to 25g/ ½ oz castor sugar per pound of salmon.

Method

 Lay the salmon flesh side up on a chopping board. Make sure the salmon is free of bones.

Mix the rock salt and the castor sugar and sprinkle generously over the salmon.

Cover the salmon with dill and pour over the whisky.

Put the gravadlax on a flat tray and cover with clingfilm. Put into the fridge for 48 hours so it is well marinated.

To Serve

Place the salmon onto a clean board and with a sharp knife cut into slanting slices. I usually allow 2 good slices each.

I like to serve with lemon slices and brown bread and butter.

This is a lovely fresh, simple, authentic first course.

Griddled Scallops with a Lime Dressing

Ingredients

18 Scallops
1 Bag of Lettuce Leaves
Olive Oil
Zest and Juice of 2 Limes

This is very much a last minute first course that is so quick and easy to prepare. It is deliciously light and tasty.

Method

First you will need to wash the scallops leaving the lovely orange coral on the scallops but discarding any membrane or black threads.

You will need a large griddle pan to which is added 3 tbsps of olive oil.

Making sure that the pan and oil are hot, cook 6 scallops at a time.

Sear for approximately 3 minutes in total, ie a minute and a half each side.

Repeat this three times keeping the scallops warm in a Pyrex dish in a very low oven.

When you have cooked all the scallops, mix in the lime juice and zest and mix well with a metal spoon.

{57}

To Serve

Arrange lettuce leaves in the middle of 6 plates and place three scallops on each plate, dividing the juices over the scallops.

Fresh Salmon and Dill Filo Parcels with Hollandaise Sauce

Ingredients
4 x 85g/ 3oz Pieces of Fresh Salmon Fillets that have been lightly smoked
4 large sheets of Filo Pastry
225g/ 8oz Butter
50g/ 2oz Dill
Zest and juice of 1 Lime
Ground Black Pepper

Method

- Melt 4oz of the butter and put aside.
- In a bowl beat the rest of the butter until soft then add the dill leaves, juice and zest of the lime and ground black pepper.
- This is a lovely zesty mixture that enhances the delicacy of the salmon.
- To assemble the parcels flour your worktop.
- Cut the filo sheets diagonally in half. You will need to do one parcel at a time.
- Put a damp tea towel over the other sheets as you work so that they do not dry out.
- With a pastry brush, cover each half sheet with melted butter.
- Now place the sheets diagonally across and place the salmon on top with a spoonful of the dill butter mixture.
- Bring each diagonal corner to corner so that you form a parcel.
- Repeat this for each parcel.
- Place on a tray and brush the remaining butter on each parcel.
- Place in the fridge until ready to cook.
- Cook for 10 –12 minutes on – 225°C/ 450°F/ Gas 7.

{58}

Hollandaise Sauce
1 tbsp White Wine Vinegar
Black Peppercorns
3 Egg Yolks
175g/ 6oz Butter – melted
Fresh Tarragon

I make my Hollandaise in the Magimix. It's easy and saves all the whisking over a pan of hot water.

Separate the eggs and place the yolks in the Magimix and blend.

Reduce the vinegar, tarragon and black peppercorns until the mixture has been reduced by half by placing in a pan over a moderate heat.

Strain into a bowl and add the liquid to the egg yolks.

Keep blending and add the melted butter slowly. The mixture will thicken to a creamy consistency.

Now place the Hollandaise in a Pyrex bowl over a pan of warm water and keep warm.

To Serve

Place your filo parcels on plates and trickle the Hollandaise Sauce round them with a large tablespoon.

Couldn't be more simple!

Smoked Trout and Pink Grapefruit Salad

Ingredients
4 Fillets of Smoked Trout
3 Pink Grapefruit – segmented
2 Avocado
Juice of ½ Lemon
Assorted Salad Leaves

Dressing
Pinch of Salt
1 tsp Caster Sugar
1 tsp English Mustard Powder
140ml/ ¼ pt Sunflower Oil
2 tbsp White Wine Vinegar
Shake together all the ingredients for the dressing in a jar. It can be kept in the fridge for 2-3 weeks.

To Assemble

- This salad looks very pretty with the pink trout and the deep pinky red colour of the grapefruits.

- Place the salad leaves on 4 plates. Scatter the trout in flake sized pieces and arrange the grapefruit segments and slices of avocado onto the salad. Pour the lemon juice over the avocado so it doesn't go brown.

- Then pour a little dressing over each salad.

- This is good served with some crusty brown bread and butter.

Smoked Trout Paté

Serves 4

{61}

Ingredients
100g/ 4oz Smoked Trout Fillet
1 tsp Horseradish Sauce
1 Egg white – whipped lightly
100ml/ 3fl oz Double Cream – whipped lightly
Pinch of Cayenne
Salt and Pepper
Juice of ½ Lemon

Method
- Lightly grease 4 ramekin dishes with olive oil, which has been put onto a kitchen towel.
- Place the smoked trout, horseradish, cayenne and lemon juice into the Magimix and process until smooth.
- Then scrap out the mixture with a spatula into a mixing bowl.
- Add the whipped cream to the trout mixture and mix well.
- Next add the whipped egg white, incorporating all the mixture.
- Add salt and pepper to taste.
- Divide the mixture into 4 ramekin dishes and leave in the fridge for 2-3 hours to set.

To Serve
- I serve this first course with lemon and cucumber slices.

To really gild the lily, some king prawns with a chive French dressing would be delicious.

SPECIAL
OCCASION
DINNER MENU

SMOKED SALMON ROULADE

. . . .

BEEF WELLINGTON

ROASTED POTATOES WITH
A HINT OF THYME

PUREE OF SPINACH
AND NUTMEG

ROASTED CARROTS AND
YELLOW PEPPERS

. . . .

HOT PASSION FRUIT SOUFFLE

Lamb

Cuts of Lamb

Fillet Lamb with a Redcurrant, Red Wine and Mint Sauce

Roast Lamb with White Onion Sauce

Spiced Lamb with Almonds and Nutty Rice

Moroccan Lamb Tagine

Lamb Shank with Roasted Root Vegetables

Lamb with a Garlic, Chestnut and Tomato Relish

Ragout of Lamb

If I had to say which roast meat I would choose as my favourite, I would always go for lamb as I love the flavour and the texture. I like lamb that has been hung for two to three weeks.

I always buy my lamb from my local butcher, John Anderson of North Berwick, who are winners of the Annual Scottish Butcher Award.

British butchers are fortunate to have quality breeds of lamb, providing different cuts of meat. Locally bred and reared lambs are Suffolk, Texel and Blackfaced breeds, and are all available in most good butchers. The lamb is usually hung in a cold store for at least 2 weeks prior to jointing.

Although I like to promote local good Scottish produce, I have to say that Wales and Cumbria have some of the best spring lamb. They seem to have woollier, thicker coats and it is lovely to see them dancing around on the lush green fields.

English spring lambs are available in June, July and August while Scottish lamb is available a bit later in August. We also have New Zealand lamb being imported in December, which is quite delicious.

Nothing beats spring lamb with Jersey Royal potatoes and baby leeks.

Cuts of Lamb

The choice cuts for roasting lamb are: -

The Leg which can be cut short or long.

The Loin which can be roasted on the bone or boned, rolled and tied up.

The Saddle which consists of two loins joined together. It is a bit harder to carve than a single loin as the backbone is retained but it is a great dinner party dish.

Rack of Lamb which consists of 6-8 rib cutlets. Your butcher can remove the chine bone (backbone). They can also trim excess fat and clean the ends of the rib bones.

This is one of the most popular cuts of lamb and is best roasted whole then cut into single cutlets.

For more economical cuts, the shoulder is good for ragout, lamb tagines, casseroles and curries.

Fillet of Lamb with a Redcurrant, Red Wine and Mint Sauce

Ingredients

6 Fillets of Scottish Lamb – 175g/ 7oz each
Olive Oil
1 Bottle of Red Wine
2 tbsps Redcurrant Jelly
1 tbsp Chopped Fresh Mint
½ tsp Cornflour mixed with 2 tbsp cold water

Method

- Preheat oven to 200°C/ 400°F/ Gas 6.
- Heat 2 tbsp of olive oil in a heavy-based frying pan and sear the fillets until brown.
- Then cook them in a roasting tin in a moderate oven for 20 minutes.

To Make the Sauce

- This can be made while the fillets are cooking.
- Pour the red wine into a large shallow pan then stir in the redcurrant jelly.
- Add the mint and stir well until the jelly is all melted.
- Then add the dissolved corn flour and mix well.
- Add salt and ground black pepper.
- When the lamb fillets are ready, take them out of the oven and rest for 5 minutes.
- Slice the fillets into 1" slices. They should be lovely and pink.
- Arrange them in the centre of each plate with a spoonful of the sauce over the lamb.

To Serve

- I think pureed spinach tastes very good with this dish and the colours go well together.

{66}

Roast Lamb with White Onion Sauce

You can buy a leg of lamb on the bone or a boned and rolled leg of lamb which your butcher can prepare for you. I prefer my lamb left on the bone as it results in more flavour.

Ingredients
1 Sprig of Thyme
1 Sprig of Rosemary
3 Cloves of Garlic
100g/ 4oz Butter
1 Leg of Lamb
Pinch of Salt and Ground Black Pepper

I always think that new minted potatoes go very well with roast lamb

Method

- Rub your lamb all over with a tablespoon of butter.
- Then make deep incisions with a sharp knife and put small pieces of garlic into each incision.
- Season the lamb with ground pepper and rock salt.
- Scatter fresh thyme and rosemary over the lamb and cover in foil.
- Cook the lamb for 20 minutes per pound weight at 200C/ 400F/ Gas 6.
- Remove the foil from the lamb for the last 30 minutes of cooking.
- Rest the lamb covered in foil for 10 minutes before carving.

{67}

I particularly like to serve a white onion sauce with the lamb. The recipe for the sauce is as follows:

Ingredients
1 Large Onion – finely chopped
50g/ 2oz Butter
1 tbsp Plain Flour
1 pt Milk
Salt, Ground Black Pepper and Ground Nutmeg

Method

- Melt the butter in a heavy-bottomed pan and add the finely chopped onions.
- Cook over a low heat until the onions are soft.
- Add the flour, stirring all the time.
- When the flour has been incorporated whisk in the milk a little at a time.
- Your sauce should be lovely and smooth.
- Lastly, season with salt, black pepper and the ground nutmeg.
- Keep the sauce warm while you carve the lamb.

{68}

BALLINDALLOCH CASTLE IN THE HEART SPEYSIDE

Spiced Lamb with Almonds and Nutty Rice

Ingredients

1 kg/ 2lb, 4oz Leg of lamb – trimmed and cubed.

2 tbsp Olive Oil

3 Cardamom Pods – crushed

Ground Cloves

1 Red Onion – finely chopped

Zest and Juice of 2 Limes

2 Cloves of Garlic – crushed

3 inch Piece of Root Ginger – finely chopped

1 tbsp Ground Cumin

250ml/ 9fl oz Natural Yoghurt (I like Yeo Valley)
+ 2 tbsps kept aside for serving with the lamb.

50g/ 2oz Ground Almonds

Fresh Coriander and Mint

For the Rice

300g/ 10½ oz Basmati Rice

50g/ 2oz Sultanas

150g/ 6oz Mixture of Toasted Pistachios and Toasted Flaked Almonds

A good pinch of fresh Coriander

This lamb dish benefits from being made a couple of days ahead and also freezes well.

Method

- Brown the lamb in 1 tbsp olive oil and set aside in an ovenproof dish.
- Heat the remaining oil and fry the cardamom and cloves.
- Add the onion, garlic and ginger and fry gently until soft.
- Then add the cumin, lime zest and juice and fry for a few more minutes.
- Add this to the lamb with the yoghurt, coriander, mint and ground almonds.
- Add 260ml /7fl oz water and cook for 2 hours at 180°C/ 350°F/ Gas 4.
- If you find it is drying out you can add a little water.

For the Rice

- Bring 1pt salted water to the boil and add the Basmati rice. Once boiling again reduce to simmer over a low heat until the rice is cooked.
- Take off the heat and drain well by running cold water through the rice.
- Put the rice into a bowl and add the sultanas, toasted pistachio, almonds and coriander and mix well.
- Place the bowl over a pan of hot water to keep warm.

To Serve

- Serve the rice with the lamb, trickling a spoonful of yoghurt over the rice.

Moroccan Lamb Tagine

Ingredients

100g/ 4oz Dried Apricots

5fl oz Hot Water

Olive Oil

1400g/ 3lbs Diced Shoulder of Lamb

2 Sticks Celery – finely chopped

3 Cloves of Garlic – sliced

1 tsp Cumin

1 tsp Coriander

1 tsp Cinnamon

1 Tin Tomatoes

275ml/ ½ pt Lamb Stock

Saffron Threads

Juice of 1 Lemon

3 tbsp Ground Almonds

4 Courgettes – cut into large pieces

1 Butternut Squash – peeled and diced

4 Large Tomatoes – skinned and quartered

Method

Preheat the oven to 180°C/ 350°F/ Gas 4

Put the apricots into a bowl and cover with hot water. Put aside for 2½ hrs.

Heat the oil in a large heavy-based pan, brown the lamb in small amounts and place into a casserole dish keeping the meat warm in a low oven until all the lamb has been browned.

Next, add the onion, garlic, and celery to the pan and continue cooking for 10 minutes.

Add the saffron, spices and lemon to the onion/ garlic mixture in the pan, then after 5 minutes incorporate well with the lamb in the casserole dish.

Add the apricots and the liquid they have been soaking in, followed by the can of tomatoes and ground almonds and mix well.

Season with salt and pepper

Place the casserole dish in an oven at 225°F/ 180°C/ Gas 4 for approximately 1¾ hours.

After an hour add the courgettes, butternut squash and tomatoes.

You may need to add a little extra water at this point.

Put back into the oven and cook for another 45 minutes.

To Serve

This is really good served with couscous. I like to buy a good quality couscous, as some varieties cook too quickly and loose the flavour. Couscous with Peppers goes particularly well with the Lamb Tagine.

Couscous with Peppers

Ingredients

2 Red Onions – finely chopped

340g/ 12oz Couscous

2 pts Boiling Water

3 Red Peppers – roasted in olive oil, skinned and chopped

2 tbsps Olive Oil

Method

Heat the olive oil in a heavy-based pan and add the chopped onions. Cook for about 5-6 minutes then stir in the couscous.

Stir for about 3-4 minutes then pour in the boiling water. Keep stirring and the water will absorb the couscous.

When the couscous is firm add the chopped roasted peppers.

Season well with salt and black pepper.

Lamb Shanks with Roasted Root Vegetables

Ingredients

3 Shanks of Lamb

1 Bottle Red Wine

Rosemary, Thyme and Ground Black Pepper

500g/ 1 lb Carrots

500g/ 1 lb Parsnips

3 Red Onions

1 Small Swede

4 Cloves of Garlic

Redcurrant Jelly

This is so easy to prepare and tastes delicious with all the flavours of the root vegetables.

I think that one lamb shank between two people is adequate, but if you are cooking this recipe for a rugby team you may want to increase the quantity of lamb shanks.

Method

- First of all place the lamb shanks in a roasting tin. Pour over the red wine and plenty rosemary, thyme and ground black pepper.
- Marinate overnight or at least for 12 hours.
- In another roasting tin assemble the vegetables.
- Slice the onions and garlic first and place in the tin.
- Next, cut the carrots, parsnips and swede into large sticks and add to the onions and garlic.
- Put the marinated lamb shanks on top of the vegetables with the red wine.
- Add 2 tbsps of redcurrant jelly.
- Cover the roasting tin with foil and cook for 3- 3½ hrs at 180°C/ 350°F/ Gas 4.

For the Rice

- I like to serve this dish on a large ashet so that everyone can help themselves. Lay the lovely vegetables on the bottom of the ashet, then the shanks and pour the juices over the top.

THE NORTHEAST COSTAL VILLAGE OF PENNAN

Lamb with a Garlic, Chestnut and Tomato Relish

Ingredients

3 Racks of Lamb – French trimmed about 900g/ 2lb in weight

3 Cloves of Garlic – crushed

1 tbsp Dijon Mustard

75g/ 3oz Pancetta – chopped

100ml/ 3½ fl oz Olive Oil

175g/ 6oz Chestnuts - roughly chopped (cooked and peeled)

75g/ 3oz Sunblush Tomatoes

2 tsp Castor Sugar

2 tbsp Balsamic Vinegar

4 tbsp Chopped Flat Leaf Parsley

Method

- Rub the garlic all over the lamb and spread the upper fat side with half the mustard.
- Put the rack of lamb in a roasting tin and press the Pancetta into the mustard.
- Drizzle the lamb with 2 tbsp of the olive oil and cook for 15-20 minutes for medium and 20-25 minutes for well done at 235°C/ 460°F/ Gas 8.
- Remove the lamb from the roasting tin and put aside to rest for 5 minutes while you make the relish.
- Put the roasting tin on a gentle heat.
- Stir in the chestnuts, tomatoes, castor sugar, balsamic vinegar, remaining mustard and olive oil into the roasting tin to make the relish. Keep stirring until well mixed.
- Season to taste.
- Carve the lamb into cutlets then stir the parsley into the relish and pour over the lamb.

I came across this recipe some time ago and adapted it to suit a commission. This was the first time that I had used chestnuts with lamb and everyone agreed that they really did go very well together. It is now very popular.

Ragout of Lamb

This recipe was given to me by a good friend who is a cook at a lovely country house in Perthshire.

Ingredients

50g/ 2oz Butter
900g/ 2lb Leg of Lamb – trimmed of any excess fat and cut into small cubes
150g/ 6oz Unsmoked Bacon
250g/ 8oz Tiny Small Shallots - peeled
3 Sticks Celery – finely chopped
3 Carrots – finely chopped
25g/ 1oz Plain Flour
½ Bottle of Red Wine
½ pt of Hot Water
500g/ 1 lb Button Mushrooms – washed
Salt and Ground Black Pepper

Method

Preheat oven to 180ºC/ 350ºF/ Gas 4.

Melt the butter in a large heavy-based pan, then add the diced lamb and cook until the meat is brown.

Remove the meat from the pan and keep warm in a Pyrex dish.

Add the bacon to the pan and cook until crispy then add to the meat.

Next, add the shallots to the pan until they are soft and golden followed by the celery and carrots.

Cook for a further 5 minutes.

Stir in the flour and gradually add the water and red wine stirring all the time until the sauce comes to the boil.

Next add the mushrooms, salt and pepper to the sauce.

Then add the meat and bacon and transfer to a large casserole dish.

Cover well and cook for 1¾ hours.

To Serve

I like to serve creamed parsnips and carrots with this ragout. It is particularly satisfying on a cold winter evening.

[77]

Beef

Beef Carbonnade

Roast Sirloin of Beef

Aberdeen Angus Fillet of Beef Wellington

Beef Casserole with Chestnuts and Redcurrant Jelly

Prime Fillet of Beef Stroganoff

Exotic Beef Curry

Beef is the meat of all large domestic cattle including Heifer, Cow, Ox and Bull. Beef cattle are specially bred for meat production with the most popular breed in Scotland being Aberdeen Angus, while in England it is the Hereford. In recent years there has been a growing demand for Highland beef which is sought after for its leanness, tenderness and low cholesterol.

When buying beef it should be red in appearance and firm and springy to the touch. It will have a network of white fat, which is described as marble. This means that there is fat in the muscle. This is important as it helps to preserve the beef as well as giving it good flavour.

The choice of cut depends on the type of dish that you are cooking. I like to use sirloin for roasting and fillet of beef, sometimes known as 'tenderloin', for beef strogonoff or chateaubriand. Diced rump steak is best for curries and blade steak for carbonnades.

Now-a-days we are much more adventurous in our experimenting with different cuisines. You can make any exotic dish with good local well-sourced produce.

Beef Carbonnade

This is a great casserole for a short lunch and very tasty.

Ingredients
2lbs Blade Steak – diced
3 tbsps Olive Oil
2 Red Onions – sliced
1 tbsp Plain Flour
2 Cloves of Garlic – finely chopped
Salt and Pepper
Ground Nutmeg
Ground Cloves
1 tbsp Castor Sugar
8 Slices of French Rustic Bread without Crusts
1 Bottle Brown Ale
½ pt hot Water

Method

{80}

- Preheat the oven to 180ºC/ 350ºF/ Gas 4.
- Heat the oil in a large earthenware pan.
- Brown the meat on both sides. Transfer to a Pyrex dish and keep warm.
- Add onions and garlic to the pan and cook until soft and slightly caramelised.
- Add the flour to soak up any remaining oil.
- Next add the brown ale and water and mix well.
- Add the ground cloves, ground nutmeg, salt and pepper.
- Cook in a moderate oven for 1½ hours.
- Before serving the Carbonnade, spread each slice of bread with french mustard and place evenly on top of the casserole, mustard side down. Push the bread down into the casserole so that it gets soaked with the meat juices.
- Remove the lid and cook for a further 15 – 20 minutes or until the bread is browned.

Delicious!

Roast Sirloin of Beef

Ask your butcher for a nice piece of sirloin that has been well hung.

Ingredients
I estimate 150g/ 6oz per person. Ask him to tie it up for you so that the meat stays intact.
Pinch of dry English Mustard
Pinch of Salt and Ground Black Pepper

Method

- Put the sirloin into a heavy-based roasting tin. Sprinkle with a grinding of black pepper, a pinch of salt and a dusting of mustard powder.
- Cover with foil.
- Cook the sirloin at 450°C/ 500°F/ Gas 7, Allowing 15 minutes per 1 lb then reducing the oven to 220°C/ 425°F/ Gas 6.
- Take the foil off the beef half way through the cooking time allowing it to brown.
- The beef should be deep pink in colour and dark brown on the outside.

To Make the Gravy

- Take the meat out of the roasting tin and leave to rest.
- Put the roasting tin on top of the oven. Brown the juices slightly and add a little hot water and a drop of red wine.
- Boil up, then pour the juices through a sieve and serve with the beef.

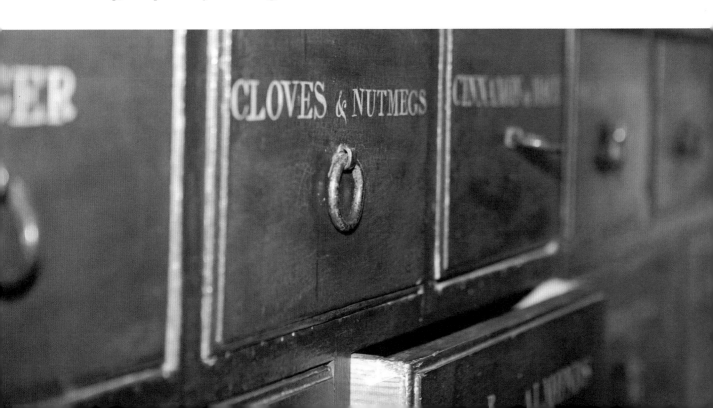

Aberdeen Angus Fillet of Beef Wellington

This is a super main course for a dinner party. It always impresses the guests.

Ingredients

1 kilo/ 3lbs Fillet of Aberdeen Angus Beef (tied with string)
1 fl oz Olive Oil
50g/ 2oz Butter
3 Shallots – finely chopped
250g/ 10oz Shiitake Mushrooms – finely chopped
Fresh Thyme
125g/ 5oz Chicken Liver Paté
375g/ 13oz Puff Pastry
1 Large Egg

Method

Preheat the oven to 220°C/ 425°F/ Gas 7.

Heat the olive oil in a large heavy-based pan.

Brown the fillet after removing the string.

Seal the meat well then place in the centre of a hot oven for 15 minutes.

Then take out of the oven and leave to cool.

Melt the butter in a pan and add the chopped shallots. Cook until soft and add the shiitake mushrooms and thyme. Set aside.

When the meat is cold, spread the paté over the top of the meat evenly with a palette knife. Then with a spoon, place the mushroom mixture on top of the paté, pressing the mixture down with a spoon. Season the top of the mushroom mixture with the salt and ground black pepper.

Roll out on a floured surface the puff pastry, making two large rectangles, each about 12" x 16 " in size.

Place the beef on one of the rectangles and place the other rectangle of pastry on top.

You may need to cut off the corners to get a neater shape. Press the sides and top and bottom with your thumb and first finger.

Make slits on top with a sharp knife and brush with a beaten egg.

For medium to rare cook at 220°C/ 425°F/ Gas 7 for 35 minutes, or for medium for 45 minutes.

Leave to rest for 10 minutes before slicing.

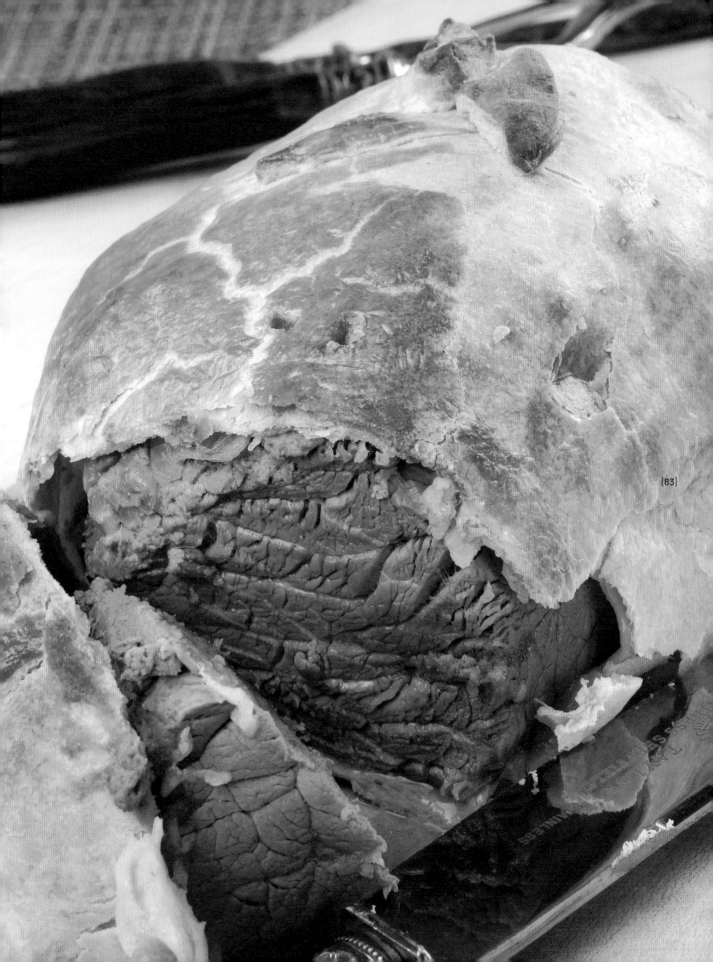

Beef Casserole with Chestnuts and Redcurrant Jelly

The redcurrant jelly complements the flavour of the beef wonderfully.

Ingredients

900g/ 2lbs Stewing Beef – trimmed and diced

1 tbsp Plain Flour with a little salt and ground black pepper

2 tbsp Olive Oil

2 Red Onions

1 Clove of Garlic – finely chopped

850ml/ 1½ pts Beef Stock

2 tbsps Redcurrant Jelly

1 Jar of Peeled and Cooked Chestnuts (420g/ 15oz)

Method

- Preheat the oven to 180°C/ 350°F/ Gas 4.
- To begin with, coat the meat lightly in the seasoned flour.
- In a large earthenware pan, heat the oil and fry the meat until browned.
- Transfer the meat into a casserole dish and keep warm.
- Add the onions to the pan and fry until soft.
- Next add the garlic and beef stock and cook for 2-3 minutes, then add this to the meat stirring well.
- Heat the red wine and dissolve the redcurrant jelly in the wine. When fully dissolved, add to the meat along with the chestnuts.
- Cook the casserole in a moderate oven for 1½ hours.

Prime Fillet of Beef Stroganoff

Ingredients

900g/ 2lbs Fillet of Beef – cut into strips

6 Red Onions – finely chopped

250g/ 8oz Small Button Mushrooms – finely sliced

50g/ 2oz Butter and 2fl oz Olive Oil

140ml/ 5fl oz Soured Cream or Crème Fraiche

Salt and Pepper

2fl oz Brandy

1 tsp French Mustard

Juice of ½ Lemon

This is a good dish to make if you have any left over bits of fillet to use up.

Method

- Melt the butter and oil and fry the beef quickly.

- Put aside and keep warm in a Pyrex dish.

- Add the onions to the pan and cook until soft. Then add the mushrooms and stir well.

- Now add the soured cream or crème fraiche and lemon juice. Stir until the cream starts to bubble.

- Put the beef back into the pan with the onions, mushrooms and cream mixture.

  Add the mustard, salt, pepper and brandy. Mix well and cook for another 5 minutes.

Exotic Beef Curry

Ingredients

2lbs Good Rump Steak – diced

2 Red Onions – finely diced

2 Cloves of Garlic – finely sliced

1 inch piece Root Ginger - finely diced

Juice of 2 Limes

3 Large Tomatoes – blanched and then remove skin and seeds and dice

3 tbsps Olive Oil

50g/ 2oz Fresh Coriander

2 tsp Ground Cumin

2 tsp Ground Coriander

2 tsp Ground Turmeric

2 tsp Marsala Curry Powder

2 tsp Cardamom Seeds

2fl oz Natural Yoghurt

50g/ 2oz Ground Almonds

1 x 15fl oz Coconut Milk

140ml/ ¼ pt Hot Water

I love this curry. It is not too hot, yet hot enough for most curry lovers.

Method

- Preheat the oven to 180ºC/ 350ºF/ Gas 4.
- Start by placing a large frying pan over a moderate heat without oil and fry the spices for 2-3 minutes.
- Put the olive oil into another pan and brown the diced stewing steak. When the steak has been browned transfer it to a casserole dish to keep it warm.
- Add the onions and garlic to the pan and cook until the onions are soft.
- Then add the root ginger and spices, followed by the limejuice.
  Mix well then add the coconut milk, diced tomatoes, ground almonds and fresh coriander and hot water.
- Add the mixture to the steak in the casserole dish and stir well.
- Cook in a moderate oven for 1½ hours.
- Remove the casserole from the oven and add the yoghurt to the curry.
- Continue to cook for another twenty minutes.

To Serve

- To complete this curry I like to serve Basmati Rice with almonds and mango chutney mixed together.
- It tastes even better made the day before. But, don't add the yoghurt until the day you are going to eat it.

{87}

Pork

Apple Sauce & Sage & Onion Stuffing

Casserole of Pork and Haricot Beans

Sticky Pork Spare Ribs

Fillet of Pork with a Mustard Sauce and Cox's Apples

How to Roast Pork

Score a loin of pork with a sharp knife, then rub salt into the skin. I don't put any butter or fat onto the skin because pork has its own fat, which in itself is enough for lovely gravy.

Cook in a moderate preheated oven 200°C/ 400°F/ Gas 6 allowing 30-35 minutes per lb. Cover the pork with foil then remove for the last 20 minutes to crackle the pork.

Roast pork always reminds me of Boxing Day in Yorkshire, with a plentiful supply of apple sauce made from Bramley apples and sage and onion stuffing. I have therefore included recipes for a delicious apple sauce and easy sage and onion stuffing.

Apple Sauce

Apple sauce is usually served cold with pork.

Ingredients
3 Large Bramley Apples
Zest of 1 Lemon
1 tsp Castor Sugar

Method

- Peel and core the apples and cut into slices then place in a heavy-based pan.
- Cover with cold water and the zest of the lemon and the sugar.
- Place over a moderate heat and cook until the apples start to fall.
- Beat the apples with a wooden spoon until you have a smooth mixture.

Sage and Onion Stuffing

Ingredients
2 tbsps Fresh Sage
1 tbsp Olive Oil
1 Onion – finely chopped
100g/ 4oz Fresh White Breadcrumbs
25g/ 1oz Melted butter
1 Whole Egg
Salt and freshly Ground Black Pepper

Method

- Mix all the ingredients together in a bowl.
- Roll into small balls and place on a greased baking tray with a spoonful of olive oil drizzled over them.
- Cook in a moderate oven for 20-25 minutes.

Casserole of Pork and Haricot Beans

Serves 6-8

Ingredients

1.4kg/ 3lbs Shoulder of Pork – trimmed and cut into cubes
5 Cloves of Garlic – crushed
7 tsp Olive Oil
2 tbsp Red Wine Vinegar
6 tbsp Brown Sugar
1 dash of Tabasco
1 tbsp Fresh Parsley
1 tbsp Oregano
1 tbsp Thyme
500g/ 1 lb Onions – finely sliced
275ml/ ½ pt Chicken Stock
2 x 15fl oz tins Tomatoes
275ml/ ½ pt Red Wine
2 x 15oz tins Haricot Beans – drain of all liquid

This casserole can be made 2 days ahead and kept in the fridge in an airtight container.

{91}

Method

- Preheat the oven to 180ºC/ 350ºF/ Gas 4.
- Cut the pork into small cubes and place in a bowl with the garlic, one third of the oil, the vinegar, sugar, Tabasco, herbs and black pepper.
- Mix well, cover and put in the fridge for 6 hours.
- Remove the pork, keeping the marinade aside.
- Heat 4 tbsp of the oil in a pan and fry the pork until it is browned on both sides.
- Place the meat in a casserole dish.
- Add the remaining oil to the pan and cook the onions until soft. Then add the stock, wine, tomatoes and the marinade and bring to the boil.
- Transfer the mixture to the pork in the casserole dish.
- Cook in a moderate oven in the covered casserole dish for 2 hours.
- Add the haricot beans 30 minutes before the casserole is ready and stir well.

Sticky Pork Spare Ribs

Ingredients

1.4kg/ 3lbs Pork Spare Ribs – your butcher can prepare these for you
3 tbsp Malt Vinegar
3 tbsp Sesame Oil
4fl oz Red Wine Vinegar
3 tbsp Clear Honey
3fl oz Soy Sauce
1 inch piece of Fresh Ginger
Juice and zest of 2 Limes
5 tbsp Muscovado Brown Sugar
1 dash of Tabasco
1 tsp Lea and Perrins Sauce

Method

- Mix all the ingredients together in a heavy-based pan. Bring to the boil and set aside.
- Leave to cool for about 1 hour.
- Place the spare ribs into a roasting tin and pour over all the marinade mixture
- Cover loosely with foil and cook in a moderate preheated oven 200°C/ 400°F/ Gas 6 for 1½ hours.
- Baste every 10 minutes to keep the ribs moist.

{92}

To Serve

- These are lovely served with a crisp green salad.

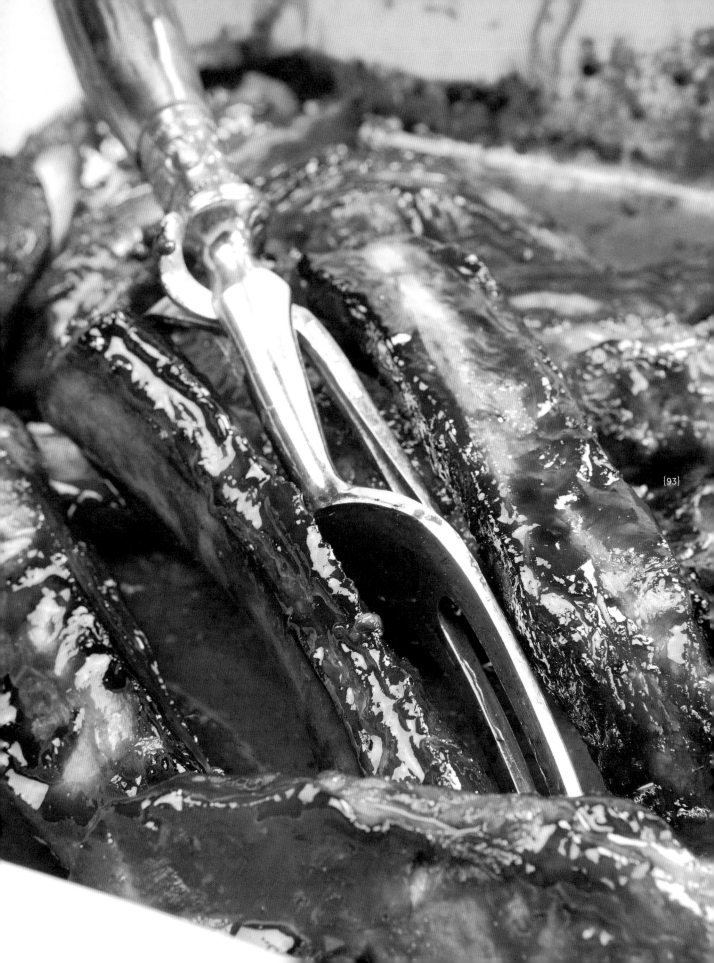

Fillet of Pork with a Mustard Sauce and Cox's Apples

Serves 6-8

Ingredients

4 Pork Fillets – cut into 16-18 discs and flattened out with a rolling pin or meat cleaver

6 Cox's Apples – with the skin and core removed and cut into 1" slices and sprinkled with the juice of 1 lemon

2 tbsp Olive Oil

50g/ 2oz Butter + 25g/ 1oz Butter for the Apples

75ml/ 3oz Brandy

2 tbsp Grainy Mustard

275ml/ ½ pt Double Whipping Cream

Black Pepper

Method

Preheat the oven to 180°C/ 350°F/ Gas 4.

Strip any fat off the pork fillet and cut into 1" discs. Put each disc between a piece of cling film and flatten with a rolling pin.

Sauté the pork discs on both sides with hot oil and melted butter in a heavy-bottomed pan.

Transfer into a covered Pyrex dish and put into a moderate oven for 30 minutes.

Next sauté the apples in a clean pan with the 1oz butter until they are a golden colour on each side. Set them aside.

To make the sauce, flame the brandy in a pan to bubbling hot temperature, then add the double cream and lastly the grainy mustard.

Season with ground black pepper.

When the pork is cooked add the juices to the sauce.

To Assemble and Serve

Put 3-4 pork fillet discs on each plate with a couple of apple rings and a tablespoon of mustard sauce.

I like to serve fresh spinach with a hint of nutmeg with this dish. The flavours complement each other beautifully.

Chicken

Stir Fried Chicken with Cashew Nuts

Chicken Breasts with Lime and Honey

Chicken with Saffron and Roasted Cherry Tomatoes

Coq Au Vin

Chicken Breasts wrapped in Parma Ham with Griddled Asparagus

Chicken has to be one of the most versatile meats. There is no substitute for fresh organic chicken sourced locally, as I really prefer the flavour.

Leftover chicken also makes excellent stock, which is a great base for soup.

{97}

Stir Fried Chicken with Cashew Nuts

Here we have a touch of the Oriental. It is very easy to prepare and is healthy too.

Ingredients
4 Organic Chicken Fillets
1 inch piece Root Ginger – peeled and sliced
1 tsp Cornflour
1 tbsp Soy Sauce
1 tsp Red Wine Vinegar
1 tbsp Dry Sherry
150ml/ ¼ pt Chicken Stock
50g/ 2oz Cashew Nuts
2 Spring Onions – chopped
2 Cloves Garlic – sliced
Juice and zest of 2 Limes
2 tbsp Olive Oil

Method

Cut the chicken into strips and put into a bowl with ginger and garlic. Put to one side.

Mix the cornflour, lime juice and zest, soy sauce, sherry, chicken stock and red wine vinegar and set to one side.

Heat a wok or large frying pan with the oil and add the chicken mixture. Cook until the chicken is tender and browned on both sides.

Add the rest of the ingredients and stir well until the mixture starts to thicken.

Lastly add the spring onions and cashew nuts. These do not need cooking. They are added to the stir-fry just before serving.

To Serve

Fine noodles go very well with this stir-fry.

Chicken Breasts with Lime and Honey

Ingredients

4 Boned Chicken Breasts with the skin left on
2 tbsps Clear Honey
Zest and Juice of 1 Lime
15g/ ½ oz Butter
85ml/ 3fl oz Chicken Stock
½ tsp Ground Ginger
½ tsp Ground Turmeric
Pinch of Salt and Ground Black Pepper

Method

Preheat oven 200°C/ 400°F/ Gas 6.

Brush the chicken with some of the honey.

Melt the butter in a large heavy-based pan. Put the chicken in the pan, skin side down and cook gently until the skin is browned.

Place the chicken in a large covered earthenware dish.

Pour the stock, honey, lime zest and juice, ginger, turmeric and salt and pepper into a pan.

Bring this to the boil and pour over the chicken breasts.

Place in the oven for 35 – 40 minutes.

Chicken with Saffron and Roasted Cherry Tomatoes

This is a great dish for a dinner party.

Serves 6

Ingredients
25g/ 1oz Fresh Thyme
25g/ 1oz Oregano
500g/ 1 lb Cherry Tomatoes on the vine
Olive Oil
6 Organic Chicken Breasts
50g/ 2oz Butter
250g/ 8oz Small Shallots – peeled
140ml/ ¼ pt White Wine
350ml/ 12fl oz Chicken Stock
3 Saffron Threads
140ml/ ¼ pt Double Cream
A pinch of Salt and Ground Black Pepper
2 Cloves of Garlic – sliced

Method
- Preheat the oven to 180°C/ 350°F/ Gas 4.
- Place the tomatoes with the garlic, thyme and oregano on a roasting tray with 1 tbsp of olive oil and roast. This will take about 10-12 minutes.
- Melt the butter in a heavy-based pan and add the seasoned chicken breasts.
- Cook on both sides to brown.
- Place them in a large earthenware dish and finish cooking in the oven for 25 minutes.
- Now add the shallots to the pan and cook until caramelised.
- Add the wine to deglaze the pan, then pour in the stock and saffron. Simmer and reduce.
- Add the cream then the chicken breasts and tomatoes.
- Simmer for another 10 minutes.
- Taste for seasoning.

To Serve
- I like to serve a puree of carrot and parsnip with this dish.

{102}

THE SPECTACULAR DRIVEWAY TO DRUMMOND CASTLE

Coq Au Vin

Ingredients

1 Large Organic Chicken – jointed plus carcass and bones

1 Whole Onion

1 Whole Carrot

A handful of Whole Black Peppercorns

125g/ 5oz Chopped Pancetta

2 medium Onions – chopped

2 sticks Celery – chopped

1 Carrot – chopped

2 Cloves garlic – sliced

2 tbsp Cognac

2 tbsp Plain Flour

½ Bottle Red Wine

Fresh Thyme

6 Bay Leaves

12 Shallots – peeled

175g/ 7oz Button Mushrooms – washed and destalked

Olive Oil

Coq au Vin is a classic French dish, which I like to make the day before. This recipe was inherited from a good friend.

Method

Preheat the oven to 180ºC/ 350ºF/ Gas 4.

Put the jointed pieces of chicken aside.

Put the carcass and bones in a pan covered with cold water.

Add the whole onion, carrot, and peppercorns and bring to the boil.

Turn the heat down then cover and simmer for 1 hour. This will give you the chicken stock.

Heat a large heavy-based pan with olive oil and cook the Pancetta until brown in colour. Remove from the pan and put into a Pyrex dish.

In the same pan, place the chicken joints seasoned with salt and pepper.

Sauté the chicken until crispy and golden brown, then remove and place with the Pancetta.

Next add 1 tbsp of olive oil to the pan and add the chopped onions, celery, carrots and garlic and fry for about 5 minutes.

Return the Pancetta and chicken to the pan.

Stir in the flour, then pour in the cognac, red wine and herbs.

Add the chicken stock slowly and continue to add it until the chicken is covered.

Bring to the boil and simmer on a moderate heat for 40-45 minutes.

Meanwhile heat 2 tbsp of olive oil in another pan. Add the shallots and cook until the shallots start to caramelise.

Then add the mushrooms and stir thoroughly.

Add the shallots and mushrooms to the chicken mixture.

As the coq au vin is simmering it will gradually thicken. Once it has, place it in the oven for the last 20 minutes.

If you make this dish the day before keep it in a cool place overnight. It can be reheated in a moderate oven 180ºC/ 350ºF/ Gas 4 for 30 minutes.

To Serve

I like to serve Coq au Vin with French green beans and little Charlotte new potatoes. Bliss!!!

Chicken Breasts wrapped in Parma Ham with griddled Asparagus

Serves 6

Ingredients
6 Chicken Breasts – organic
6 Large Slices of Parma Ham
12 Asparagus Spears – trimmed
2 tbsp Olive Oil
100g/ 4oz Butter
1 tbsp Plain Flour
140ml/ ¼ pt Milk
275ml/ ½ pt Chicken Stock
½ tsp Ground Nutmeg
Pinch of Salt and Ground Black Pepper

Method

- Preheat oven to 180°C/ 350°F/ Gas 4.
- To start, trim any fat off the parma ham and wrap each slice round a chicken breast.
- Heat a large frying pan with 2oz of the butter. When the butter is hot, place the chicken, ham side down, into the pan.
- Sauté until the ham is crispy then turn the chicken over for a further 2-3 minutes.
- Remove the chicken and place in a large earthenware dish and put in a moderate oven for 25 minutes.
- To make the sauce, melt the rest of the butter, whisk in the flour then add the milk and chicken stock. Whisk well until you have a smooth consistency.
- Then add the ground nutmeg, salt and black pepper.
- Lastly, heat a large griddle pan with the olive oil and add the asparagus spears until they are crispy on both sides.
- It is better to do this in batches so that they crisp more evenly.

To Serve

- Cut the chicken diagonally into 4 slices. Pour a little sauce on top. Then place 2 asparagus spears over each chicken.
- This is a lovely summer dish, especially when served with a green salad, avocado and basil.

Game

{107}

Venison

Venison is the name given to the meat of any deer. In the United Kingdom this can be Roe, Red, Fallow and Sika. Roe Deer is considered to be the tenderest, followed by Red and Fallow Deer. The hanging of a carcass of venison should be about 10 days.

The largest of the Red Deer is usually found in the Highlands of Scotland, Cumbria, Norfolk and parts of South West England.

{108}

Fallow Deer can be found in Forestry ground in both England and Scotland. The season for Fallow Deer in England is 1st August to 28th February. In Scotland the dates are 1st August to 15th February.

Roe deer are mainly found in Scotland and East Anglia. The season is slightly different to that for Fallow Deer. In England the dates are 1st April to 31st October and in Scotland 1st September to 31st March.

Venison is dark in colour with very little fat. Due to the lack of fat, the meat will shrink when cooking and may need some additional fat when roasting. While the fillet is very good pan-fried, the haunch and saddle are the parts of the deer used for roasting.

Venison is becoming more available due to the promotion of deer farming on a commercial level. Most game dealers are able to supply venison prepacked to good major and specialist food outlets.

Venison will freeze well up to a year.

Venison with Redcurrant and Chestnuts

Ingredients

1.5kg/ 3lb Haunch of Venison – cut into small chunks

2 tbsp Seasoned Plain Flour

4 tbsp Olive Oil

2 Onions – thinly sliced

3 Parsnips – cut into thin strips

3 Carrots – cut into thin strips

3 Sticks of Celery – finely diced

1 Clove Garlic – skinned and chopped

1 Bottle Red Wine

3 tsp Redcurrant Jelly

200g/ 8oz Unsmoked Back bacon – diced

1 x 15oz Tin of Chestnuts – cooked and peeled

Method

Preheat the oven to 180ºC/ 350ºF/ Gas 4.

Toss the venison in the seasoned flour.

Heat a heavy-based pan with the oil and brown the meat all over.

You will need to do this in 3 to 4 batches.

Place the meat in a casserole dish.

Sauté the bacon in the pan for 2-3 minutes then add to the venison.

Next put the onions in the pan and cook for a few minutes.

Then add the carrots, celery, parsnips and garlic. Cook for about another 5-10 minutes until the vegetables are soft.

Add the red wine and redcurrant jelly.

Lastly drain the chestnuts of any liquid and add to the pan.

Add all this mixture to the venison and bacon.

Stir well and cook for 1½ - 1¾ hours

This is best made a couple of days in advance. Once cold transfer to an airtight container and keep in a larder or fridge.

Fillet of Venison with Port Sauce and Shiitake Mushrooms

Serves 4-5

A full flavoured dish, this is lovely for a winter dinner party when venison is in plentiful supply.

Ingredients

5kg/ 1 lb Fillet of Venison – cut into 1 inch slices
1 tsp Fresh Thyme
2 tbsp Olive Oil
8 Small Shallots
1 Clove Garlic – sliced
1 tbsp Redcurrant Jelly
275ml/ ½ pt Port
200g/ 8oz Shiitake Mushrooms
Chopped Parsley
50g/ 2oz Butter

Method

- Heat the olive oil in a large heavy-based pan and fry each slice of venison for 2-3 minutes until brown.
- Keep warm in a Pyrex dish.
- Add the shallots, garlic and thyme to the pan and fry until the shallots start to caramelise.
- Next add the port and redcurrant jelly and reduce the liquid by half.
- In another pan melt the butter and when hot add the mushrooms. When they are cooked add the chopped parsley.

To Serve

- Arrange 2-3 slices of venison on each plate with a spoonful of the shallot wine mixture round the venison. Finally, place a few mushrooms on top of the venison.

Roast Haunch of Roe Deer

Ingredients

1 Small Haunch of Venison– I prefer roe deer as it is particularly tender and moist

For the Marinade

2 tbsp Olive Oil + 3 tbsps for sealing

275ml/ ½ pt Red Wine

1 Onion – sliced

25g/ 1oz Fresh Thyme

50g/ 2oz Juniper Berries

1 Clove Garlic – sliced

For the Sauce

1 Onion – finely sliced

2 Carrots – finely diced

2 Sticks Celery – finely diced

2 tbsp Red Wine Vinegar

50g/ 2oz Butter

Delicious for a shoot weekend dinner, only a light first course and a pudding are required as it is so wonderfully rich and flavoursome.

{113}

Method

- Preheat oven to 170°C/ 325°F/ Gas 3.
- Place the venison in a large casserole dish and arrange the bacon slices evenly on top of the venison.
- Mix all the marinade ingredients together and pour over the venison.
- Cover and leave for 12-14 hours or overnight.
- Wipe the venison dry and seal it on both sides in a large roasting tin on top of the hob in 3 tbsps of oil.
- Strain the marinade from the casserole dish and add it to the roasting tin.
- Cover the roasting tin with foil and cook in a low oven for 3½ hours.

To Make the Sauce

- Take the venison out of the roasting tin and keep warm.
- Sieve the juices
- Cook the vegetables in butter and when soft add to the juices.
- Then add the red wine vinegar.
- Sieve again into another saucepan and you should have a lovely rich sauce.

To Serve

- I like to serve red cabbage with red onion and Cox's apples with this haunch of venison.

Pheasant

Pheasant is probably the most recognisable of all game birds. You are more likely to see a pheasant on a country lane, roadside or green field than any other game.

Pheasant is probably the most recognisable of all game birds. You are more likely to see a pheasant on a country lane, roadside or green field than any other game.

The hen is the smaller bird and not as colourful as the cock. The feathers of the hen are mainly beiges and browns while the cock pheasant is the larger of the two with green glossy feathers and a deep shinny chestnut chest.

In my opinion, it is the most delicious of all game birds. Young pheasant are good for roasting and older pheasants make delicious casseroles.

The season for pheasant is October 1st to February 1st. This is a shorter shooting season than for partridge. A young pheasant shot in October generally needs to hang for 3 days. Later in the season, January – February, the birds should be hung for 1-2 weeks. They should always be hung on their own, from their necks down.

When buying pheasants, they are usually presented by the brace. This means one cock and one hen. Many people prefer a hen to a cock as the meat is regarded to be more flavoursome. However, young cocks are delicious when roasted.

Hen pheasants usually serve 2 people and a cock pheasant will generously serve 3.

Pheasants can be kept in the freezer for up to 9 months.

Pot Roast Pheasant

This is a good way of cooking pheasants that are still available at the end of the pheasant season. It is very simple to prepare and warming in the winter months.

Ingredients

2 Pheasants

2 Red Onions – peeled and quartered

2 Parsnips – cut into large chunks

2 Carrots – cut into large chunks

2 Leeks – sliced

1 Small Swede – diced

1.8 ltrs/ 3¼ pt Game Stock

1 tsp Oregano

1 tsp Thyme

500g/ 1 lb Maris Piper Potatoes – peeled and cut into chunks

Salt and Ground Black Pepper

Method

- Preheat the oven to 190°C/ 375°F/ Gas 5.
- Place the pheasants in a large casserole dish and add the vegetables, stock and herbs.
- Place in the centre of the oven and cook for approximately 2¼ hours.
- Check half way through and turn the pheasants over. You may need to add a little more stock.
- Add salt and pepper to taste.

{115}

Pheasant Breasts with Fennel

Ingredients
2 Large Pheasants
100g/ 4oz Butter – unsalted
200g/ 8oz Fennel – cut into fine strips
2 Large Shallots
1 Garlic Clove – peeled and crushed
150ml/ ¼ pt White Wine
300ml/ ½ pt Pheasant Stock (made from 2 Onions, 1 Bay Leaf and 2 Carrots)
Juice of ½ Lemon
150ml/ ¼ pt Double Cream
1 tbsp Chopped Parsley
1 tbsp Chopped Chives
Pinch of Salt and Black Pepper

Method

Preheat the oven to 200°C/ 400°F/ Gas 6.

First of all remove the breasts carefully from the birds.

Then place the pheasant carcasses and legs in a pan with the onions, carrots and bay leaf. Cover with cold water, bring to the boil and simmer for 1 hour.

Heat 50g of the butter and cook the fennel in a large heavy-based pan until soft. Put aside.

Keep warm in the oven.

Add the pheasant breasts to the pan and cook for 3-4 minutes on each side.

Then transfer the pheasant breasts to a baking tray and cook for a further 15 minutes.

Melt the remainder of the butter in the pan, add the shallots and when they start to soften add the crushed garlic. Continue to cook for 4-5 minutes.

Then pour in the wine and reduce the liquid. Next add the double cream, pheasant stock and lemon juice. Bring to the boil and bubble for 5-6 minutes. Add the chives and parsley, season with salt and pepper and mix well.

To Serve

Divide the fennel between 4 plates. Cut the pheasant breasts into 4 slices and place the 4 slices on top of the fennel. Trickle the sauce round the breasts, being quite generous as the sauce really does enhance the flavour of the fennel.

Devilled Pheasant

Ingredients
Cooked Pheasant from 2 birds

For the Sauce
150ml/ ¼ pt Double Cream
2 tsp Medium Curry Powder
Dash of Worcester Sauce
Dash of Tabasco
2 tbsp Mango Chutney
Dash of Cayenne Powder

Method

Heat the oven to 200°C/ 400°F/ Gas 6.

Simply slice the cold pheasant and layer it into a shallow ovenproof dish.

Mix all the sauce ingredients together, then pour over the pheasant. Place the dish in the oven and cook for 20 mins until the sauce is bubbling.

To Serve

I like to serve this with Basmati Rice and an avocado, cucumber, mint and tomato salsa.

This is a good recipe to use up left over cooked pheasant. You can also do this dish with left over chicken as well.

Partridge

Partridge is considered to be the real McCoy of game birds. In September and the early part of October, young partridge have a dark beak and yellow coloured legs. The older birds have a paler grey beak, grey legs and a more rounded feathers whereas the young partridges have pointed feathers.

The shooting season for partridge is 1st September to 1st February. Early in the season, in autumn, partridge should only be hung for 3-4 days. Later on in the season, with more severe weather conditions, they should be hung for a week so that the cool air can circulate them evenly.

Partridge are best served young and at this age are excellent for roasting. Older ones are suitable for slow cooking casseroles and are very good in a mixed game pie.

Partridges can be kept up to 7 months in the freezer.

THE BREADALBANE FOLKLORE CENTRE OVERLOOKING THE FALLS OF DOCHART AT KILLIN

Partridges with Apples and Grapes in a Drambuie Sauce

Serves 10

Ingredients
5 Partridges – cut in half
2 pts Double Cream
100g/ 4oz Green Seedless Grapes
3 Cox's Apples – skin left on and cut into chunks
2 Small Glasses of Drambuie
Pinch of Paprika
Juice of 1 Lemon

This is a delicious dinner party dish that is very easy to prepare.

Method
- Preheat oven to 180°C/ 350°F/ Gas 4.
- I allow 1 partridge between 2 people as it served in a rich sauce. You can always add more partridge according to their size if you prefer.
- Place the partridge in a shallow, ovenproof dish and cover with the cream.
- Then cover with foil and cook slowly for 1½ hours.
- After cooking for 45 minutes, add the green grapes and apple chunks.
- Then add the paprika and lemon juice and mix well.
- Half an hour before serving, mix in the Drambuie.

To Serve
- This dish keeps well and is lovely with fine green beans and duchess potatoes.

Roast Partridge

Ingredients
4 Young Partridge
8 Rashers of Smoked Streaky Bacon
9 Onions – quartered
75g/ 3oz Butter
Salt and Black Pepper

Method

- Preheat the oven to 200°C/ 400°F/ Gas 6.
- Season the birds with salt and pepper and smear the butter over the birds.
- Tie two rashers of bacon across the breast of each bird.
- Put the birds into a roasting tin, cover with foil and place in the oven.
- Then after 20 minutes remove the foil to make sure the bacon is nice and crispy.
- Place the birds in an ashet and pour the juices over them.

To Serve

- Game Chips are a very good accompaniment.

{123}

Game Chips

- You will need 500g/1lb of potatoes and Sunflower Oil for deep-frying.
- Peel the potatoes then slice them very finely. If you have a Magimix it comes with a very fine slicer, which does the job extremely well.
- When sliced, thoroughly dry the chips on a clean teatowel.
- Fry in deep hot oil. Move them around once or twice to stop them from sticking.
- Drain well and serve with the partridge.

The best way to cook young partridge is to simply roast it with some smoked bacon and butter. October and November are the best months for young partridge.

Partridge Casserole

This is a good lunch time recipe; ideal for a shooting lunch.

Ingredients
1 tbsp Olive Oil
5g/ 2oz Butter
2 Partridges – cut in half lengthways
6 Shallots
2 Carrots
2 Parsnips – finely diced
2 Celery Sticks – finely chopped
3 Rashers of Smoked Streaky Bacon – finely chopped
150ml/ ¼ pt Red Wine
275ml/ ½ pt Game Stock
2 tbsp Redcurrant Jelly
Salt and Pepper

To thicken casserole make Beurne Marnie
25g/ 1oz Butter
50g/ 2oz Plain Flour.
Just knead these together with your hands.

Method

- Preheat the oven to 150°C/ 300°F/ Gas 2.
- Heat the oil and butter together and gently brown the partridges in a heavy-based casserole dish.
- When browned remove the partridges onto a separate plate.
- Then add the onions to the casserole dish, followed by the carrots and parsnips, then the celery and the bacon. Cook for 5 minutes.
- Put the partridges back into the casserole dish and add the game stock, red wine and redcurrant jelly, salt and pepper.
- Cook this in the oven for approximately 1 hour, then gently thicken the sauce with a whisk adding the beurre marnie till sauce thickens.

{125}

Roast Woodcock

As woodcock are a lot more of a rarity than pheasant, partridge and other game, they are best cooked simply, with some good quality brandy or white wine.

Ingredients
2 Woodcock – cleaned and trussed
2 Rashers of Smoked Bacon
2 Slices of White Bread
50g/ 2oz Butter
1 Glass White Wine or Brandy
3 tbsp Olive Oil
1 tsp Plain Flour
Lemon Wedges and Watercress

Method

- Preheat the oven to 220°C/ 425°F/ Gas 7.
- Place the birds in a small roasting tin and smear each bird with the butter.
- Then place a rasher of bacon over the woodcock.
- Cover the roasting tin with foil and cook for 30 minutes.
- Next, take off the foil and spoon the juices over the birds and cook for a further 10 minutes.
- Take the crusts off the bread and cut into 2 circles with a large scone cutter. Fry the bread in the oil until golden brown on both sides.
- When the woodcock are ready, put the bread croutes on 2 plates and place the woodcock on top.
- Whisk the flour into the juices and add the wine or brandy.
- Add salt and pepper to taste.
- Pour over the woodcock.

To Serve
- Serve with a garnish of watercress and lemon wedges.

Pigeon with Rowan Jelly and Red Wine in a Herb Sauce

Ingredients

4 Small Pigeons
4 Rashers Smoked Streaky Bacon
100g/ 4oz Washed Whole Button Mushrooms
8 Small Shallots
50g/ 2oz Plain Flour
2 tbsp Rowan Jelly
150ml/ ¼ pt Red Wine
275ml/ ½ pt Game Stock
Salt and Pepper
1 Large bunch of Fresh Herbs including Parsley, Thyme, Mint, Coriander, Oregano
2 tbsp Cognac

{129}

Method

- Preheat the oven to 170°C/ 325°F/ Gas 3.
- Making sure the pigeons are clean and ready for the oven, place one rasher of bacon over each pigeon.
- Heat the butter in a large casserole dish and fry the pigeons until golden brown in colour.
- Remove the pigeons to a plate and set aside.
- Fry the shallots in the casserole dish until caramelised, then add the button mushrooms.
- Stir in the flour and cook out for 2 to 3 minutes.
- Gradually stir in the stock and red wine.
- Place the pigeons back into the casserole dish and add the herbs, salt and pepper.
- Place a tight lid on the casserole dish and cook for 1½ hours.
- When ready. Strain the sauce into a saucepan for a smooth mixture then lastly add the cognac.

To Serve

- Pour a little sauce over the pigeons and serve the rest of the sauce in a sauceboat.

I like to serve some spinach leaves and a little creamed potato with the pigeon.

Duck Breasts with Rowan Jelly, Port and Orange Sauce

(Garnished with poached kumquats)

Ingredients

4 Small Duck Breasts
2 tbsp Rowan Jelly
150ml/ ¼ pt Port
Juice of 1 Orange
1 tsp Cornflour – dissolved in 2 tbsp water
1 tbsp Olive Oil
Salt and Pepper
8 Kumquats or 2 Clementines quartered
50g/ 2oz granulated sugar

Method

- Preheat the oven to 200°C/ 400°F/ Gas 6.
- First of all place the duck breasts on a chopping board with the breast side up.
- Now trim the duck by taking off any excess fat from the sides with a sharp knife, removing any sinew or bobbles of fat.
- There shouldn't be any fat left on the meat at all.
- Now heat a large shallow pan with the olive oil.
- Rub the skin on the duck breasts with salt and place skin side down into the pan.
- Cook until the skin is golden brown and then place in a roasting tin to cook in the oven for 15 minutes.
- It will be lovely and pink after that time, but if you prefer it more well cooked leave it in the oven for another 5 to 10 minutes.

To Make the Sauce

- Dissolve the rowan jelly in the port with the orange juice and simmer for 5 minutes.
- Then carefully add the dissolved cornflour and cook out for another 2 to 3 minutes.

To Make the Kumquat Garnish

- Melt the sugar in ¼ pt of cold water.
- Cut the kumquat into small pieces leaving on the stalk.
- Poach them gently in the syrup. You may like to add ½ juice of a lemon depending on how sweet you like the syrup.

This is a real dinner party dish that has the wow factor. Kumquats are available at good supermarkets and specialist food and vegetable outlets

To Serve

When the breasts are ready, place them on a clean board and cut them skin side up diagonally, and place on plates.

Trickle the lovely rowan jelly sauce over the duck breasts with a spoonful of the kumquats on the side.

Little new roast potatoes and some braised fennel go particularly well with this dish.

Roast Duck with Black Cherries

This is a traditional recipe for duck. It is easy to prepare as you can make the stuffing ahead of time.

Ingredients
1 x 4½ lbs Duck
Pinch of Salt

Stuffing
25g/ 1oz Butter
1 Red Onion- finely chopped
100g/ 4oz Chestnuts – chopped
(You can also buy good ones in a
tin by Epicure)
100g/ 4oz Good Quality White Breadcrumbs
1 tbsp Crushed Thyme
1 tsp Chopped Sage

Pinch of Paprika
Pinch of Cinnamon
Salt and Ground Black Pepper
Grated Rind of 1 Lime
Juice of ½ Lime
1 Beaten Egg

Sauce
500g/ 1 lb Tin of Black Cherries
in their Juice (Already stoned)
3 tbsp Red Wine Vinegar
2 tsp Cornflour

{132}

When cooking duck you need to cook it at 15 minutes per lb. plus 15 minutes over to be pink, or if you prefer it more well done change it to 20 minutes per lb.

Turn the duck over halfway through the cooking time and reduce the temperature to 180°C/ 350°F / Gas 4 for the remainder of the time.

Method

- Preheat the oven to 200°C/ 400°F/ Gas 6.
- First of all you will need to make the stuffing.
- Heat the butter and gently fry the onion until soft and transparent.
- Then mix all the ingredients in a large bowl combining everything together evenly.
- Lastly add the beaten egg.
- Put the stuffing into the cavity of the duck and place in the roasting tin.
- Sprinkle the duck with salt.
- Cover the roasting tin with foil and place in the centre of the oven. Remove the foil half way through the cooking time.
- When the duck is cooked put it onto a large ashet to keep warm.

To Make the Sauce

- Remove all the fat from the roasting tin and add a little hot water to the tin to deglaze.
- Add vinegar and the juice from the cherries.
- Blend cornflour with 2 tsps of cold water and add to the mixture.
- Bring to the boil, stirring all the time
- Finally, add the cherries and cook for another 2-3 minutes.

To Serve

- Carve the duck onto an ashet. Garnish with some watercress and serve the sauce separately.

I like to serve this tasty dish with creamy potatoes and glazed carrots.

{133}

BLUEBELLS

Game Pie

Ingredients

500g/ 1 lb Diced venison – tossed in flour

4 Pheasant Breasts – keep the carcasses for the stock

4 Partridge Breasts – keep the carcasses for the stock

6 tbsp Olive Oil + 50g/ 2oz Butter

500g/ 1 lb Button Mushrooms

250g/ 8oz Pancetta – chopped

3 Onions – chopped finely

½ Bottle Red Wine

2 Cloves Garlic – finely chopped

1 tsp Fresh Parsley

1 tsp Fresh Tarragon

2 tbsp Redcurrant Jelly

Pinch of Salt and Black Pepper

300ml/ ½ pt Stock made from pheasant and partridge carcass + 2 onions

Bay leaf and 2 Carrots

500g/ 1 lb Puff Pastry – I use ready made. Saxby's is the best.

1 Egg

I like to make this dish the day before because it benefits from all the flavours mingling together and maturing. The taste really does improve being made in advance.

Method

- Preheat oven to 200°C/ 400°F/ Gas 6.
- First of all prepare the stock by placing all the stock ingredients into a large pan, cover with water and simmer for an hour.
- Cut the pheasant and partridge breasts into cubes and fry off in a large frying pan with 3 tbsp of olive oil. Cook until sealed then place in a large casserole dish.
- Next, fry the floured venison until browned evenly and add to the pheasant and partridge.
- Add the butter and the rest of the olive oil to the frying pan followed by the onions and garlic. When soft, add the Pancetta and lastly the button mushrooms.
- Add all this mixture to the casserole dish.
- In a clean pan mix together the strained stock, red wine and redcurrant jelly. Once the jelly is dissolved add the parsley and tarragon.
- Add this to the casserole and season with salt and black pepper.
- Cook for 2 hours.
- Leave overnight in a cool place and the mixture will thicken up nicely.
- Place the mixture into a large pie dish. Cook for a further 40 minutes then leave to cool for 20 minutes.
- Roll out the pastry onto a floured surface.
- Wet the edge of the pie dish with water and gently place the pastry over the pie mixture.
- Trim the edges neatly. There should be enough pastry to make a few leaves for the centre of the pie.
- Quickly beat the egg with a fork and brush the top of the pie with a pastry brush.
- Bake at 225°C/ 425°F/ Gas 7 for 25-30 minutes.

Fish

Luxury Fish Pie

Halibut with Cherry Tomatoes and Thyme

Sea Bass with Garlic, Lime and Herbs

Poached Salmon with Cucumber and Dill Sauce

Salmon Fillets with Honey, Soy Sauce and Ginger

Trout with Toasted Almonds

Cooked Lobster with a Chive and Lemon Mayonnaise

We are so lucky in Scotland to have such a great choice and availability of fresh fish and in such plentiful supply, both from our rivers and seas.

Luxury Fish Pie

Ingredients
1 Fillet of White Haddock
2 Fillets Undyed Smoked Haddock
1 Fillet of Cod- skinned
6 Scallops
250g/ 8oz Cooked and Peeled Prawns
2 Hard Boiled Eggs – chopped
1 tbsp Chopped Parsley
250g/ 8oz Button Mushrooms
3lbs Maris Piper Potatoes – peeled and cut into chunks
1 tbsp Olive Oil

For the Fish Sauce
100g/ 4oz Butter
100g/ 4oz Plain Flour
550ml/ 1 pt Milk
50g/ 2oz Butter – for potatoes
25g/ 1oz Butter – for sautéing mushrooms
Salt, Ground Black Pepper and Pinch of Nutmeg

Method
- Preheat the oven to 225ºC/ 450ºF/ Gas 8.
- First of all cut the haddock, smoked haddock and cod into chunks removing any bones and place in a pan with the 1 pint of milk.
- Bring the milk to the boil, simmer for 5 minutes then take the pan off the heat.
- Next heat the 1 tbsp of olive oil in a heavy-based frying pan. Add the scallops which should have any black membrane removed and cook for 1½ minutes on each side and put them in a dish until the sauce is made.
- Wash and slice the button mushrooms, heat the 25g/ 1oz butter and sauté the mushrooms then add the chopped parsley.
- Melt the 100g/ 4oz butter in the heavy-based pan, whisk in the flour, then add the strained milk that the fish has been cooked in.
- Mix to a smooth consistency.
- Then add the chopped hard-boiled eggs, mushrooms and parsley, the cooked haddocks, scallops and prawns.
- Season with salt and ground black pepper.
- Transfer to an earthenware dish and leave to cool.
- Cook the potatoes until soft then strain. Mash with a potato masher, add the butter, pinch of salt, ground black pepper and a pinch of nutmeg.
- Beat well with a wooden spoon.
- Spread the potato on top of the fish mixture and cook in a hot oven for 25-30 minutes or until the potato is browned.

One of my favourite supper dishes which can be made the day before. It is so fresh and tasty that you can savour the goodness with every mouthful. This recipe is particularly delicious with the addition of fresh local scallops which I'm able to get from the Firth of Forth.

Halibut with Cherry Tomatoes and Thyme

Serves 6

Ingredients
6 x 125g/ 5oz Halibut Fillets
1 Small punnet Cherry Tomatoes
A few sprigs of Fresh Thyme
Juice of 1 Lime
2 Cloves Garlic – finely sliced
3 tbsp Olive Oil

Method

- Preheat the grill to a moderate heat.
- Cover your grill tray with foil.
- Place the halibut fillets on the foil and sprinkle over them the garlic and loose fresh thyme (taken off the sprigs).
- Divide the lime juice and olive oil between the halibut and dot the cherry tomatoes around the tray.
- Allow just 10-12 minutes to cook.

To Serve

- This is a lovely dish served with creamy potatoes and petit pois.

One of my favourite fish is halibut and here is a very simple recipe for it

Sea Bass with Garlic, Lime and Herbs

Ingredients

175g/ 7oz Sea Bass Fillets
Zest and Juice of 3 Limes
4 tbsps Mixture of Dill, Parsley and Mint
3 tbsps Olive Oil
2 Cloves Garlic – finely chopped
Pinch of Salt
Ground Black Pepper

For the Dressing

Juice of 2 Lemons
1 tsp Chopped Tarragon
2 tsp Olive Oil
Ground Black Pepper

Method

{141}

- Preheat the grill.
- You will need a large tray covered in foil.
- Make deep incisions onto the skinside of the sea bass fillets. Place them onto the foiled tray.
- Mix the lime zest and juice, garlic, herbs and olive oil. Place the mixture carefully into the incisions.
- Pour the rest of the mixture over the fish.
- Place the fillets skinside down under the hot grill and turn over once the fish starts to cook.
- It should take just 10-15 minutes to cook.
- Mix all the dressing ingredients together.

To Serve

- Place the sea bass onto individual plates and then pour over the dressing.
- This is a delicious meal ideally served with a crispy green salad with some avocado tossed in.

Poached Salmon with Cucumber and Dill Sauce

Ingredients

6lbs Salmon which has been gutted
Mixture of 2 lemons, handful of Parsley and Black Peppercorns
1 Glass White Wine

For the Sauce

½ Cucumber – cut into small cubes
1 tbsp Dill – taken of its stalks
50g/ 2oz Butter
50g/ 2oz Plain Flour
2 tbsp Double Cream
Pinch of Salt and Ground Black Pepper

To Decorate

1 Lemon – thinly sliced
¼ Cucumber – sliced thinly and cut in half

{143}

Method

- Preheat oven to 170°C/ 325°F/ Gas 3.
- If you have a fish kettle half fill it with water. Place it on the hob and when it starts to come to the boil add the fish, lemons, parsley, peppercorns and white wine.
- Bring to the boil and cook for 5 minutes per pound. Turn off the heat and leave to sit in water for 20 minutes.
- If you don't have a kettle, use a large tray with water and the other ingredients and place in oven for approximately 1 hour. Then leave to cool.
- Empty the water from the kettle or tray and skin the salmon. Put it on a large ashet or oval plate.

For the Sauce

- Melt the butter then add the flour and whisk in the milk.
- Next add seasoning followed by the double cream.
- Just 5 minutes before serving add the cucumber and dill do as not to discolour it.

To Serve

- Decorate the salmon with lemon slices and cucumber but serve the lovely flavoured sauce separately. This is an ideal dinner party main course which looks beautiful in the centre of the table.

Salmon Fillets with Honey, Soy Sauce and Ginger

Serves 4

Ingredients

4 Salmon Fillets
2 tbsp Olive Oil
4 tbsp Soy Sauce
2 tbsp Runny Honey
1 inch piece of Root Ginger- peeled and cut into thin strips
Juice of 1 Lime
1 Spring Onion – topped and tiled and cut into thin strips
1 Yellow Pepper – deseeded and cut into thin strips

Method

- Preheat oven to 180°C/ 350°F/ Gas 4.
- Place the salmon fillets into a roasting tin.
- Divide the lemon juice between the salmon with a good grinding of black pepper and add the olive oil.
- Mix the rest of the ingredients in a large bowl and spoon evenly over the salmon.
- Place in the oven for 15-20 minutes, basting the sauce over the salmon halfway through the cooking time.

To Serve

- When ready, I would serve on individual plates with lemon wedges and some fine noodles.

{144}

This is a lovely Oriental way of cooking salmon that doesn't need too much preparation.

Trout with Toasted Almonds

This is one of the most classical ways of serving trout.

Ingredients
5 Fresh Trout – cleaned and gutted
1 tbsp Plain Flour
75g/ 3oz Flaked Almonds
Juice of 1 Lemon
75g/ 3oz Butter
Lemon Wedges and Parsley to serve

Method

Gently roll the trout in the flour. Shake off any excess flour.

Heat a frying pan without any butter and add the almonds, stirring until they are golden brown. Put into a bowl. They don't need any added fats as the nuts have their own natural oils.

Now add butter to the pan and gently fry the trout for approximately 5-6 minuets on each side until golden brown.

Arrange on the plates with the lemon wedges and parsley. Sprinkle the almonds on top of the trout.

What could be better? Quite delicious, particularly with fresh trout straight from the river.

Cooked Lobster with Chive and Lemon Mayonnaise Serves 4

The best times to have lobsters are the months that don't have an R in them – May, June, July and August. I simply like to cook and serve them cold with a delicious mayonnaise and salad.

Ingredients
4 x 1½ lbs live Lobsters

For the Mayonnaise
Juice of 1 Lemon
25g/ 10oz Chives – very finely chopped
1 Whole Egg and 1 Egg Yolk
2 tbsp White Wine Vinegar
140ml/ ¼ pt mixture of light Olive Oil and Sunflower Oil
½ tsp Colmans English Mustard Powder
Pinch of Salt and good grinding of Black Pepper
½ tsp Caster Sugar

Method
- Fill a fish kettle with water and bring to the boil. If you don't have a fish kettle, a large pan with a tight fitting lid will be just as adequate.
- Place the lobsters in the boiling water and boil for a good ten minutes.
- Take the lobsters out of the water and place on a tray to leave to cool.
- Once they have cooled right down, place the lobsters face down on a clean chopping board. With a sharp pointed knife split them down the centre.
- You will see a sac near the head. This will need to be removed. If there are any black treads or membrane remove them.
- Take the lobster out of the shell, give it a quick wash and cut into pieces. Place back into the shell.
- Crack the claws. I use a rolling pin wrapped inside a teatowel for this. Then you can easily pick out the flesh and place the lobster meat back into the shells ready to serve.

To Make the Mayonnaise
- Put the egg, egg yolk, mustard powder, salt, sugar and black pepper in the Magimix. Blend and then add the white wine vinegar. After the vinegar has been incorporated, slowly blend in the oils, a spoon at a time.
- Transfer the Mayonnaise to a bowl, add the lemon juice and the chives and stir well.

To Serve
- Serve lemon wedges and cucumber slices with the lobster and a generous spoonful of mayonnaise.
- I also like to serve a crunchy green salad as an accompaniment to the lobster.

Vegetarian

Tomato, Leek and Cheese Puff

Gnocchi with Spinach and Goats Cheese

Asparagus and Mushroom Risotto

Asparagus and Camembert Tart

Crunchy Vegetable Stir Fry

Tomato, Leek and Cheese Puff

This is a very simple lunch dish

Ingredients
1 Large Sheet of Ready Rolled Puff pastry
3 Large Leeks
Pinch of Salt
½ tsp English Mustard Powder
100g/ 4oz Grated Gruyere Cheese
50g/ 2oz Grated Isle of Mull Cheddar
1 Small Tub of Cherry Tomatoes
1 Whole Egg – beaten

Method

Preheat the oven to 200ºC/ 400ºF/ Gas 6.

Place the puff pastry on a large, greased 8" swiss roll tin.

Slice and cook the leeks in salted hot water until soft.

Drain well then place evenly onto the puff pastry.

Sprinkle the mustard powder over the leeks.

Cut the tomatoes in half and place over the leeks.

Mix together the Gruyere and Cheddar and place over the leek and tomato mixture.

Brush the edges of the pastry with the beaten egg.

Cook for 20 minutes or until the pastry is cooked and well risen.

Gnocchi with Spinach and Goats Cheese

Ingredients

300g/ 1¼ lbs Potato Gnocchi

Handful of Fresh Sage and Fresh Basil

3 tbsp Olive Oil

250g/ 8oz Fresh Spinach

200ml/ 7fl oz Single Cream

Juice of 1 Lemon

1 Clove Garlic – sliced finely

100g/ 4oz Soft Goats Cheese – cut into cubes

50g/ 2oz Parmesan – grated

1 tsp Ground Nutmeg

Salt and Ground Pepper

Method

- Preheat the oven to 190ºC/ 375ºF/ Gas 5.
- Boil water in a heavy-based pan with a pinch of salt then add the potato gnocchi with the sage and basil.
- Cook until the gnocchi is well risen. Strain and put aside.
- Next, put 1½ tbsp of the olive oil in a large frying pan and add half the spinach and garlic with a grinding of black pepper and nutmeg.
- Cook the spinach until it begins to wilt. Put it into a bowl.
- Heat the rest of the olive oil with the remaining garlic, spinach, black pepper and nutmeg. When cooked add to the spinach that has been set aside.
- Beat together the single cream, lemon juice and goats cheese.
- Mix the spinach and potato gnocchi together and transfer to a large earthenware dish.
- Pour over the goats cheese mixture and sprinkle parmesan on top.
- Cook for 20 minutes or until the mixture is bubbling.

To Serve

- A tomato and basil salad complements this dish perfectly.

{154}

Potato gnocchi can be sourced from most supermarkets and delicatessens.

Asparagus and Mushroom Risotto

Ingredients

6 tbsp Olive Oil

1 pt Vegetable Stock (refer to page 24)

500g/ 1 lb Arborio Rice

500g/ 1 lb Chestnut and Shitake
Mushrooms – sliced

2 Red Onions – finely chopped

3 Cloves Garlic – finely sliced

½ pt White Wine

500g/ 1 lb Trimmed Small Asparagus Spears

2 tbsp Parmesan Cheese – grated

1 tsp Chopped Chives

Pinch of Salt and Ground Black Pepper

Method

- Heat the oil in a large heavy-based pan.
- Add the onions and garlic and cook until soft.
- Then add the asparagus spears and mushrooms and cook for 2-3 minutes before adding the rice.
- Add the rice, cook for 3-4 minutes.
- Next add the wine and cook for a further 1-2 minutes.
- Then add the vegetable stock and finish cooking until the rice is cooked and the liquid reduced.
- Lastly add the chives, black pepper and salt.
- Before serving, add the Parmesan cheese.

Asparagus and Camembert Tart

Serves 6

Ingredients
250g/ 8oz Plain Flour
125g/ 5oz Diced Unsalted Butter
25g/ 1oz Parmesan Cheese – grated
Pinch of English Mustard Powder
500g/ 1 lb – Trimmed Asparagus Spears
3 Whole Eggs
2 Egg Yolks
175g/ 6oz Camembert – cut into small cubes
2 tsp Fresh Chopped Chives
275ml/ 10fl oz Double Cream
Pinch of Nutmeg
Pinch of Salt and Ground Black Pepper

Method

- Preheat the oven to 190ºC/ 375ºF/ Gas 5.
- Mix the flour, butter, Parmesan and mustard powder in the Magimix. The mixture will come together in the form of a ball of dough.
- Press the mixture in a loose-bottomed, greased 9" tartlet tin and place in the fridge for 30 minutes.
- Bake blind in the oven for 15 minutes.
- Take out of the oven and put aside to cool.
- Blanch the asparagus in hot water then drain well.
- Place them attractively in the tartlet tin.
- Mix together the egg yolks, whole eggs, double cream, nutmeg, salt and ground black pepper.
- Mix well until everything is combined.
- Pour this mixture over the asparagus.
- Then add the cubes of Camembert and sprinkle over the chives.
- Cook for 20-25 minutes.

Crunchy Vegetable Stir Fry

Ingredients

4 tbsps Olive Oil

3 tbsps Soy Sauce

250g/ 8oz Carrots – cut into sticks

1 Yellow Pepper and 1 Red Pepper – cut into thick strips

250g/ 8oz Baby Corn

2 Red Onions – finely sliced

3 Cloves Garlic – finely sliced

500g/ 1 lb Button Mushrooms – sliced

1 inch Ginger – finely sliced

4 Spring Onions – finely sliced

2 tbsps Sunflower Seeds

Zest and Juice of 1 Lime

Method

- Heat the oil in a large frying pan.
- Sauté the onions, garlic, ginger and spring onions and cook until onions are soft.
- Add the carrots and peppers and cook for a further 3-4 minutes.
- Then add the baby corn and mushrooms.
- Stir well then add soy sauce and lime zest and juice.
- Lastly stir in the sunflower seeds.

To Serve

- This is lovely served with fine noodles.

{157}

Scottish
Carrots

Scottish
Mushrooms
95p per kg

Scottish Ca
Bunches
£1·50 each

Scottish Beetroot
Bunches

Scottish Beetroot
Bunches

Scottish
Cauliflower

Scottish S
Cabbages
95p e

Vegetable Accompaniments

Here are some popular vegetable accompaniments that go very well with the main course recipes.

Buttered Spinach

Puree of Carrot and Parsnips

Braised Red Cabbage with Onions, Cox's Apples and Cloves

Braised Fennel with Shallots and Garlic

Griddled Asparagus

Sautéed Broccoli with Red Onion, Ginger and Chillies

Broad Beans in a White Sauce

Roasted Carrots and Orange Peppers

Baby Leeks and Bacon

Roast Potatoes

Roasted New Potatoes with Rosemary and Garlic

Dauphinoise Potatoes

Buttered Spinach

░ My favourite vegetable of all time in leafy green spinach.

░ Simply put washed spinach in a large pan. Add a very small amount of boiling water.

░ When the spinach starts to bubble, drain into a colander. Really squeeze out the water with a wooden spoon, as it will be too watery otherwise.

░ Put the spinach back into the pan over a very low heat and add a good knob of butter, a generous grinding of black pepper and a sprinkling of fresh nutmeg.

░ Place in a Pyrex or earthenware dish, cover with foil and keep warm in a very low oven.

Puree of Carrot and Parsnips

░ Peel and chop two thirds of carrots to a third of peeled and chopped parsnips.

░ Put into a pan, cover with cold water and add a pinch of salt.

░ They need to be boiled until they are really soft.

░ Drain well. Then place the drained carrots and parsnips into the Magimix machine or any kind of blender.

░ Add a good knob of butter, a pouring of single cream, ground black pepper and a pinch of mace.

░ Blend well until you get a lovely smooth puree.

░ Keep warm in a covered dish.

{161}

Braised Red Cabbage with Onions, Cox's Apples and Cloves

░ This red cabbage is particularly good with venison, or any gamey meat. It is also quite delicious served cold.

░ Slice a red cabbage thinly, taking off the outer leaves and the core.

░ Place in a large shallow dish and cover with boiling water for 3 to 4 minutes and then drain off the water.

░ This softens the cabbage before cooking.

░ In a medium pan melt the butter and add 2 chopped onions, ground cloves and mace.

░ When the onions are soft, add 3 Cox's apples, chopped with their skins on but the core and pips taken out. Cook out for 2 to 3 minutes.

░ Next add a tablespoon of muscavado brown sugar, and a ¼ pt of red wine vinegar.

░ Pour the mixture over the cabbage and cook in a moderate oven at 190°C/ 375°F/ Gas 5, for 45 minutes, stirring halfway through the cooking time.

░ This also freezes well.

Braised Fennel with Shallots and Garlic

- I like fennel in the winter as it is such a warming vegetable with a unique taste of its own.
- Cut the fennel bulbs into 6 pieces. Place the pieces into a roasting dish.
- Peel the cloves of garlic and add to the fennel.
- Next, peel 12 small shallots and sauté them in olive oil until caramelised and add to the fennel.
- Add 2 tablespoons of olive oil and ¼ pt of white wine to the fennel. Cook in a moderate oven for 40-50 minutes at 190°C/ 375°F/ Gas 5.

Griddled Asparagus

- Asparagus is at its best in June, July and August, although it is available all year round in supermarkets from countries such as Peru and Spain.
- I like to griddle asparagus as it gives a nice crunchy texture.
- You will need a small griddle pan with deep ridges.
- Place over a moderate to high heat.
- Heat a drop of olive oil and when hot and add the asparagus, cooking half an inch apart. Turn so that it is evenly crispy on all sides. This will take 5 to 10 minutes.

Sautéed Broccoli with Red Onion, Ginger and Chillies

You will need

3 Heads of Broccoli

1 inch piece of ginger, peeled and cut into very small dice

2 red onions, peeled and finely sliced

1 red chilli, finely diced

3 tablespoons of olive oil

- First of all cut the broccoli into large florets and blanche in salted water for 2-3 minutes. Then drain and put aside.
- Heat the olive oil in a large heavy-based pan and sauté the onions for 3-4 minutes. Add the ginger and the chilli and cook till the ginger is soft.
- Then add the broccoli florets, mix well and cook for 5 minutes until the broccoli is crunchy and a caramelised golden colour.

Broad Beans in a White Sauce

750g/ 1½ lbs Broad Beans

For the Sauce you will need
50g/ 2oz Butter
50g/ 2oz Plain Flour
550ml/ 1 pt Full Fat Milk
Salt and Pepper

You will need to shell the broad beans once you have taken them out of their pods. It is a bit fiddly but the outer shell can sometimes be tough and it is well worth the extra time.

To Make the Sauce

Melt the butter, whisk in the flour, and continue to whisk over a low heat for three to four minutes to cook out the flour. Slowly add the milk until you get a lovely smooth consistency. Season with salt and pepper.

Cook the broad beans in salted boiling water for 3-4 minutes. Drain well. Mix the beans with the sauce and add a tablespoon of freshly chopped parsley.

Roasted Carrots and Orange Peppers

Preheat the oven to 220°C/ 425°F/ Gas 7.

Peel 500g carrots and cut them into chunky sticks. Cut four orange peppers into wide strips, omitting all the seeds and stalk.

Place 4 tablespoons of extra virgin olive oil plus 1 tablespoon of castor sugar into a roasting tin then add the carrots and the peppers.

Mix well and roast for 40 –45 minutes, stirring halfway through.

Baby Leeks and Bacon

Cut 10 baby leeks that have been washed thoroughly. Put them into a pan of cold water and bring to the boil. Simmer for 3 – 4 minutes then drain.

Grill 6 rashers of unsmoked bacon until crispy, then cut with scissors into small dices. Add some chopped parsley and a knob of butter. Mix the bacon mixture with the leeks.

This is very good with roast pork or any game dish.

Roast Potatoes

- I like to use Maris Piper or King Edward Potatoes for roasting. They are very flavoursome and have a very good texture for roasting.
- Preheat your oven to 220°C/ 425°F/ Gas 7.
- Cut 1 kg of peeled potatoes into chunks, place in a pan and cover with salted water. Bring to the boil and simmer for 8 –10 minutes then drain into a colander until every trace of water had gone.
- Place into a roasting tin with 3 tablespoons of goose fat or a covering of sunflower oil and a sprinkling of sea salt. Roast them on the top shelf of the oven turning them over halfway through the cooking. Cook for 1 hour until crisp and golden brown.

Roasted New Potatoes with Rosemary and Garlic

- Preheat the oven to 220°C/ 425°F/ Gas 7.
- Put 3 tablespoons of olive oil and 3 finely copped cloves of garlic into a roasting tin. Add 750g/ 1½ lbs baby new potatoes and lashings of rosemary. Add a few generous grinds of black pepper and mix well together. Roast for 35–40 minutes tossing halfway through.
- These potatoes are very good with roast lamb, with my preference being King Edward or Maris Piper potatoes.

Dauphinoise Potatoes

- These are quite calorific but delicious and very much a special occasion potato dish.
- Preheat the oven to 190°C/ 375°F/ Gas 5
- With the Magimix slicing disc, you will need to slice 900g/ 2lbs peeled potatoes. Layer them in a buttered roasting tin. Add 4 cloves of finely crushed garlic, sea salt and a liberal amount of ground black pepper.
- Cover with double cream then scatter freshly grated Parmesan over the top of the cream. This will need to be cooked for 1 - 1½ hours and you should end up with a lovely golden brown gratin top.
- This will serve 4 – 6 people.

A SUMMER
DINNER
PARTY MENU

CADO MOUSSE WITH PRAWNS

. . . .

FILLET OF LAMB WITH
REDCURRANT, RED WINE
AND MINT SAUCE

BABY NEW POTATOES

JULIENNE OF CARROTS
AND ASPARAGUS SPEARS

. . . .

HAZELNUT MILLE-FEUILLE
WITH A RASPBERRY
COULIS

Puddings

Hazelnut Mille-Feuille with a Raspberry Coulis

White Chocolate Mousse with Nectarine and Raspberry Coulis

Lemon Mousse with Almond Macaroons

Chocolate Almond Cake

Passion Fruit Soufflés

Brandy Baskets with Coffee Ice-cream

Strawberry Ice-cream with Shortbread Crescents

Gooseberry Ice-cream

Ginger and Chocolate Ice-cream

Hot Chocolate Soufflés with Scottish Berried Fruit

Raspberry Cream Patisserie Tartlets

Exotic Pineapples

Raspberry and Kiwi Pavlova

Lemon and Lime Roulade with a Strawberry Cream Filling

Chocolate Mousse

Hazelnut Mille-Feuille with a Raspberry Coulis

Serves 8

Ingredients
8 Egg Whites
250g/ 10oz Castor Sugar
5oz Ground Almonds
Drop of Vanilla Extract

Crème Patisserie
2 Egg Yolks
75g/ 3oz Castor Sugar
½ tsp Vanilla Extract
25g/ 1oz Cornflour
275ml/ ½ pt Double Cream

Raspberry Coulis
250g/ 8oz Local Scottish Raspberries
2 tbsps Sieved Icing Sugar
100g/ 4oz Raspberries for decoration
Handful of Fresh Mint

Method

- Preheat oven to 150°C/ 300°F/ Gas 2.
- Grease 3 x 8" swiss roll trays and line with parchment paper.
- Whisk the egg whites stiffly then gradually add the castor sugar a teaspoon at a time.
- The mixture should stand in peaks.
- Fold in the vanilla extract and ground hazelnuts with a metal spoon. Stir evenly combining all the mixtures together.
- Place a tablespoonful of the meringue mixture onto the trays. You should get about 9 spoonfuls on each tray.
- Cook the meringues for 1-1¼ hours. They should be crispy on the outside and soft in the middle. Place on a cooling wire.

To Make the Crème Patisserie

- Heat the cream and vanilla in a heavy-based pan, but do not boil.
- In a bowl whisk together the egg yolks, castor sugar and cornflour.
- Add the cream to the egg and sugar mixture and whisk well.
- Return to the pan and whisk thoroughly over a low heat.
- The mixture will thicken and look like creamy custard.
- Place in a bowl and cool completely.

To Make the Raspberry Coulis

- Put the raspberries and sieved icing sugar into the Magimix and blend well.
- Put the mixture through a sieve into a bowl. The result should be a lovely smooth puree.

To Assemble and Serve

▨ You will need 3 meringue discs per person.

▨ Put ½ teaspoon of the crème patisserie on each disc and on the top disc decorate with a raspberry and sprig of mint.

▨ Trickle the raspberry coulis round the plate.

▨ I like to finish the presentation with a dusting of icing sugar.

I love this pudding. It is a wonderful dinner party dessert. The taste is delicious and it looks very attractive if you want to impress your guests.

White Chocolate Mousse with Nectarine and Raspberry Coulis

Serves 4

Ingredients
25ml/ 1fl oz Whole Milk
100g/ 4oz White Chocolate – chopped
2 Drops Vanilla Extract
1 Drop Mint Extract
2 large Eggs – separated
1 tbsp Castor Sugar
1 Sachet Gelatine – dissolved in 1 tbsp of hot water
100ml/ 3½ fl oz Double Cream – whipped

Method

- Heat the milk in a heavy-based pan and add the chocolate. Stir over a low heat until the chocolate is melted.
- Then add the vanilla extract and mint extract and stir well.
- In a bowl beat the egg yolks and sugar until they are pale and creamy then add the dissolved gelatine.
- Add the chocolate mixture and mix thoroughly so that the gelatine is evenly incorporated.
- Place the mixture in a bowl, cover with cling film and put in the fridge to thicken for 1 hour.
- Once thickened, remove from the fridge and fold in the double cream that has been whipped.
- Next, whisk in the egg whites until they stand up in peaks and fold into the mixture quickly.
- Transfer the mixture into a pretty dessert bowl and when set, cover the mousse with cling film.

The tartness of the coulis really contrasts with the sweetness of the mousse. We are very lucky here in Scotland to have an abundance of locally grown raspberries.

Raspberry and Nectarine Coulis

This is a delicious summer pudding, but watch out, because it is very moreish and you will want more.

Ingredients
2 Nectarines
250g/ 8oz Fresh Raspberries
2 tbsps Sieved Icing Sugar
1 tsp Fresh Mint

Method

- Skin the nectarines and put all the flesh in the Magimix along with the raspberries, icing sugar and mint.
- Whizz up until the nectarines are all squashed down.
- Then strain the coulis through a sieve into a bowl.

To Serve

- I like to serve the mousse in a pretty china dish or crystal bowl, with the lovely raspberry and nectarine coulis in a jug.

Lemon Mousse with Almond Macaroons

Ingredients

Juice and Zest of 2 Lemons

Zest of 1 Lime

1 Sachet Gelatine – dissolved in 3 tbsps hot water

275ml/ ½ pt Double Cream – whipped lightly

3 Eggs – separated

75g/ 3oz Castor Sugar

½ a Lemon - cut into thin slices for decoration

Method

First of all dissolve the gelatine in hot water and set aside.

Whisk the egg yolks and castor sugar until thick and pale, then add the lime zest, lemon juice and zest and whisk again until thick.

Fold in the gelatine and mix thoroughly.

Add the whipped cream and lastly the egg whites, whisk stiffly. Incorporate the whites evenly so that you have a smooth mixture.

Transfer to a glass or soufflé dish and chill in the fridge for 3-4 hours.

This is a classic pudding that has the advantage that you can make it in advance.

Macaroon Biscuits

Ingredients

1 Large Egg White

125g/ 5oz Castor Sugar

75g/ 3oz Ground Almonds

1 tsp Plain Flour

Drop of Vanilla Extract

50g/ 2oz Flaked Almonds

Method

Preheat the oven to 170ºC/ 325ºF/ Gas 3.

You will need 2 x 8" swiss roll trays greased and lined with parchment paper.

Mix together the sugar and ground almonds.

Add the egg white and beat vigorously.

Next add the plain flour and vanilla and beat well.

Spoon a teaspoonful of the mixture at a time onto the trays.

Place a flaked almond on top of each macaroon.

Cook for approximately 10-12 minutes until crispy on the outside.

Cool on a wire tray.

To Serve

Decorate the mousse with lemon slices and serve with the macaroon biscuits, which contrast beautifully with the smoothness of the mousse.

Chocolate Almond Cake

Although this is a cake, it does very well as pudding as it is lovely; moist and gooey.

Ingredients
75g/ 3oz 70% Dark Chocolate - chopped
25g/ 1oz Milk Chocolate – chopped
2 tsps Instant Coffee Powder
2 tbsps Brandy
1 tsp Vanilla Extract
50g/ 2oz Ground Almonds
50g/ 2oz Plain Flour
100g/ 4oz Unsalted Butter
75g/ 3oz Castor Sugar
2 Large Eggs

Dark Chocolate Glaze
2fl oz Double Cream
100g/ 4oz 70% Dark Chocolate
50g/ 2oz Toasted Flaked Almonds

This is delicious with whipped cream

Method
- Preheat the oven to 180°C/ 350°F/ Gas 4.
- Grease and line a 9" loose-bottomed round cake tin.
- Melt both chocolates in a bowl over a pan of hot water and stir until smooth.
- Stir the coffee into the chocolate.
- Add the brandy and vanilla extract, mix well and set aside to cool.
- Combine the flour and ground almonds together. Cream the butter and sugar until light and fluffy.
- Add the eggs one at a time, beating well into the chocolate mixture. Add the sugar and butter mixture and give it a really good beating.
- Pour the mixture into the tin and bake for 30-35 minutes.
- It should be firm on the outside and moist and soft in the middle.

For the Glaze
- Heat the cream in a heavy-based pan. When it starts to boil take it off the heat.
- Add the chocolate and beat until thick and glossy. Cool for 20 minutes.

To Serve
- Spoon the glaze over the cake with a palette knife and decorate with toasted almonds.

Passion Fruit Soufflés

This soufflé has the most exquisite taste, refreshing and zesty.

Ingredients
Zest of ½ Lime
2 Ripe Passion fruits
2 Eggs – separated
150g/ 6oz Castor Sugar
1 Drop Vanilla Extract

For the Ramekin Dishes
25g/ 1oz Melted Butter
1tsp Castor Sugar

Method

Preheat the oven to 220ºC/ 425ºF/ Gas 7.

Grease the ramekin dishes with the melted butter and sprinkle in the 25g castor sugar.

Scoop out all the flesh of the passion fruit and put through a sieve into a bowl. Be careful not to let any pips fall through.

Whisk the egg yolks and castor sugar until thick and pale, then add the zest of ½ lime and a drop of the vanilla extract. Whisk until well incorporated.

Fold in the passion fruit juice.

Whisk the egg whites until they are standing in oft peaks and fold into the passion fruit mixture.

Divide into the ramekin dishes.

Cook for 10-12 minutes. By which time they should be well risen and firm around the edges.

Dust with icing sugar.

{177}

Brandy Baskets with Coffee Ice-cream

I love the smoothness of the ice-cream in the crunchy brandy baskets. A really yummy pudding and much easier to make than you might imagine.

Ingredients
100g/ 4oz Butter
100g/ 4oz Granulated Sugar
125g/ 5oz Golden Syrup
100g/ 4oz Plain Flour
1 level tsp Ground Ginger
Juice of ½ Lemon

Method

- Preheat oven to 170ºC/ 325ºF/ Gas 3.
- You will need 2 x 8" baking trays greased and lined with parchment paper.
- You will also need 2 small teacups or dariole moulds buttered on the outside to mould the baskets.
- Melt the butter, sugar and golden syrup in a heavy-based pan over a moderate heat. Stir until the sugar is dissolved and the butter is melted.
- Place the flour, ground ginger and lemon juice in a bowl. Add the syrup mixture to it and beat well. Leave to rest for 5-10 minutes.
- Place dessert spoons of the mixture on to the baking trays. Each tray should have just 2 dessert spoons as the mixture spreads. Place in the oven and watch carefully.
- The mixture will start to bubble and turn a golden brown colour. This will take roughly 10-12 minutes to cook.
- To lift the cooked mixture off the trays, you will need a palette knife or a fish slice greased with butter. Lift off gently and place over the teacup moulds.
- Repeat this until the mixture is finished.
- Place the baskets on a wire tray when they are moulded.
- If you feel that the biscuit mixture is getting hard before moulding the basket, just pop it back in the oven to soften the mixture.
- This may sound tricky, but once you get the hang of it, it is so easy.

Coffee Ice-cream

Ingredients
1 tsp Vanilla Extract
2 Egg Yolks
150g/ 6oz Castor Sugar
850ml/ 1½ pts Double Cream
2 tsp Cold Coffee – made from real coffee. I use the Italian La Vazza Ground Coffee

Method

- Whisk the egg yolks, vanilla extract and sugar together until thick and pale.
- Place the cream and coffee together in a heavy-based pan and heat slowly without boiling.
- Add the cream and coffee to the egg mixture and place in a Pyrex bowl over a pan of hot water. Whisk continually until really thick.
- Place in a plastic container and put in the freezer.
- When it is half way frozen take out of the freezer and beat well, then place back in the freezer.

To Serve

- I put a tiny bit of whipped cream on the base of the plate for the brandy basket to sit on, so it won't wobble around the plate.
- It also looks pretty with 2 or 3 orange segments placed on the base of the plate around the basket.
- Put one dollop of coffee ice-cream into each basket and you are in pudding heaven.

{179}

Strawberry Ice-cream

This is a good recipe for using up any strawberries that have gone slightly soft.

Ingredients
150g/ 6oz Strawberries – roughly chopped
2 Large Egg Whites
75g/ 3oz Castor Sugar
110ml/ 4fl oz Double Cream – lightly whipped

Method
- Whisk egg whites until stiff then gradually add the castor sugar.
- Then mix in the strawberries and lastly the double cream.
- Make sure the mixture is evenly incorporated.
- Transfer to a plastic container and place in the freezer.
- Remove and beat well after 1 hour.
- Return to the freezer but remove 20 minutes before eating.

Method
- This is delicious with little shortbread crescents.

Shortbread Crescents

These shortbread crescents are delicious with ice-creams and mousses.
They freeze very well in an airtight container or a tin.

Ingredients

150g/ 6oz Unsalted Butter (chilled)
150g/ 6oz Sieved Plain Flour
75g/ 3oz Castor Sugar = 25g/1oz for rolling out the mixture
75g/ 3oz Ground Rice

Method

- Preheat the oven to 150ºC/ 300ºF/ Gas 2.
- You will need 2 x 8" baking trays greased and lined with parchment.
- Put all the ingredients into the Magimix.
- They will whizz up and form a ball.
- Lift out and place on a work surface.
- Scatter castor sugar on the work surface and a rolling pin and roll out until the mixture is quite thin.
- You may have to do this a couple of times.
- Now cut the mixture with a small scone cutter.
- Again with the cutter cut the shortbread rounds in half. You will get two different shaped biscuits, which makes it more interesting.

{181}

TRANQUIL AND PRISTINE BEACH ON THE WESTERN ISLE OF BARRA

Gooseberry Ice-cream

Ingredients

500g/ 1 lb gooseberries
Zest of 2 Limes and Juice of 1 Lime
75g/ 3oz Castor Sugar
4 Large Eggs – separated
100g/ 4oz Sieved Icing Sugar
300ml/ ½ pt Whipped Double Cream

This ice-cream is gorgeous and keeps for ages in the freezer.

Method

- Put the gooseberries in a pan with the zest and juice and castor sugar. Do not add any water as the natural juice from the gooseberries will seep out.

- Remove from the heat when the gooseberries are soft.

- Blend in the Magimix /or blender and put through a sieve into a bowl. This takes a bit of time, but is paramount to the success of the ice-cream.

- Leave to cool.

- Whisk the egg whites until stiff then add half the icing sugar until the mixture looks meringue like. Then transfer to a large bowl.

- Whisk the egg yolks with the remaining icing sugar until it is pale and thick.
  Softly whip the cream.

- Mix the egg yolk and cream mixture together. Then add the cooled gooseberry puree to the egg and cream mixture. Mix well.

- Lastly, fold in the meringue mixture so the components are well incorporated.

- Place in a plastic container and put in the freezer. Beat well after one hour and return to the freezer.

{182}

I always think it is a shame that the gooseberry season is so short. Gooseberries are a most delicious fruit.
We are also very lucky north of the Border to have lots of fruit farms, so good quality fresh fruit is so easy to obtain virtually on the doorstep.

Ginger and Chocolate Ice-cream

Ingredients

100g/ 4oz 70% Dark Chocolate

4 tbsps Ginger Wine – I use Crabbies Ginger Wine

2 Pieces of Stem Ginger – cut into very small pieces

2 egg whites

125g/ 5oz Demara Sugar

4 tbsps Water

225ml/ 8fl oz Double Cream

Zest of 1 lemon

This is a very good ice-cream that I sometimes serve with poached pears.

Method

- Put the chocolate, ginger wine and lemon zest into a Pyrex bowl over a pan of hot water.
- Stir until the chocolate is melted then lift off the heat and put aside.
- Whisk the egg whites until they form soft peaks.
- Dissolve the demara sugar in the water over a low heat then increase the heat to bring to the boil. Boil rapidly for 1-2 minutes.
- Quickly add the sugar mixture to the egg whites, whisking all the time.
- Continue whisking until it is cool and thick, forming a meringue mixture.
- Fold in the stem ginger.
- Whisk the double cream and then fold into the meringue mixture.
- Lastly, fold in the cooled chocolate mixture into the meringue and cream. Mix well.
- Freeze for several hours or overnight in a large plastic container.
- Give the ice-cream another good stir two hours after placing it in the freezer.

Hot Chocolate Soufflés with Scottish Berried Fruits

Ingredients

250g/ 10oz Mixed Berries – raspberries, blueberries, blackberries
5 Large Eggs – separated
½ tsp Coffee Granules
250g/ 9oz 70% Dark Chocolate – I like to use Menier or Lindt
50g/ 2oz Castor Sugar
1 Drop Vanilla Extract
275ml/ ½ pt Double Cream

For Decoration
A few sprigs of mint and Icing Sugar

For Greasing Ramekin Dishes
25g/ 1oz Castor Sugar and 25g/ 1oz Melted Butter

For all you chocolate lovers out there, this recipe is to die for. It is pure chocolate heaven.

{185}

Method

- Preheat the oven to 220ºC/ 425ºF/ Gas 7.
- Grease 6 ramekin dishes with butter and a sprinkling of castor sugar.
- Mix all the berried fruits together and place in a bowl. Cover with cling film and leave in the fridge.
- Put the coffee granules, chocolate and double cream into a large heavy-based pan.
- Place the pan over a low heat and stir until the chocolate is melted.
- Mix the egg yolks, vanilla extract and castor sugar together in a large bowl. Add the melted chocolate mixture to the eggs and sugar and beat well.
- Beat the egg whites, preferably with an electric whisk, until the mixture is standing up in peaks.
- Fold the egg whites into the chocolate mixture with a metal spoon.
- Make sure it is well incorporated and that there are no traces of egg white.
- Place boiling water into a roasting tray then fill the ramekin dishes with the soufflé mixture. Cook for 25 minutes or until well risen.

To Serve

- While the soufflés are cooking, you can decorate the side of each plate with the mixed berries. I like to put a sprig of mint on top of the fruit to make it look pretty. When the soufflés are ready, place a soufflé on each plate and lastly dredge over some icing sugar.
- I like to serve double cream with this.

Raspberry Crème Patisserie Tartlets

Ingredients

For the Pastry Cases
150g/ 6oz Sieved Plain Flour
100g/ 4oz Unsalted Chilled Butter
1 tsp Sieved Icing Sugar

For the Crème Patisserie
2 Egg Yolks
275ml/ ½ pt Double Cream
½ tsp Vanilla Extract
75g/ 3oz Castor Sugar
1 tbsp Cornflour

To Decorate
2 Large Punnets of Raspberries
1 Sprig of Mint

Method
- Preheat the oven to 170ºC/ 325ºF/ Gas 3.
- Whizz up the pastry ingredients and mould into 6 small tartlet tins.
- Bake blind for 20-25 minutes.
- Place on a cooling tray and leave until cool.

For the Crème Patisserie
- Mix together in a bowl the egg yolks, vanilla extract, castor sugar and cornflour.
- Heat the cream in a pan over a low heat, without boiling, then pour over the egg yolk mixture and whisk well.
- Return the mixture to the pan and whisk well until it thickens.
- Remove from the heat straightaway then put into a clean bowl and leave to cool.

To Assemble and Serve
- Place one tartlet on each plate and spoon in the cream mixture.
- Then place the raspberries neatly on top, covering all the cream mixture.
- Place a mint leaf on top with a dredging of icing sugar.
- You can assemble this about 20 minutes before serving.

Exotic Pineapples

This is a healthy option, full of goodness and vitality. However, if you want to be naughty, you can serve it with cream.

Ingredients

3 Small Pineapples
2 Passion Fruit
1 Small Mango – cut into small discs
100g/ 4oz Scottish Logan Berries
1 Kiwi – peeled and sliced thinly
1 Charantais Melon – cut into small dices (This is an orange flesh melon)
100g/ 4oz Blueberries

Method

Cut the pineapples in half lengthways, leaving the stalks on.

With a sharp knife, discard the core from the centre of each half pineapple.

Then remove the rest of the pineapple and cut it into small chinks and place in a bowl. Keep the shells to be used as bowls.

Cut the passion fruits in half and scoop out the flesh and add to the pineapple.

Add the diced mango and melon, then the sliced kiwi and the berries.

Mix gently with a metal spoon.

To Serve

Divide the prepared fruit into the 6 pineapple shells. This looks very Hawaiian with the stalks on the pineapple. It is very easy to prepare and would suit either lunch or dinner.

{187}

Raspberry and Kiwi Pavlova

Serves 6

This was my father's all time favourite pudding. It came out at every family occasion. It is particularly good in the summer when we have such a large abundance of berries. You can always substitute raspberries for strawberries or blueberries.

Ingredients

4 Large Eggs
250g/ 9oz Castor Sugar
1 Drop Vanilla Extract
½ tsp White Wine Vinegar
1 Large Punnet of Raspberries
3 Kiwi Fruits – peeled and cut into slices
275ml/ ½ pt Whipped Double Cream

Method

Preheat the oven to 130ºC/ 250ºF/ Gas 1.

Line an 8" x 10" baking tray with greaseproof or silicon paper.

Whisk the egg whites, preferably with an electric beater, until stiff.

Continue to whisk gradually adding the castor sugar a spoonful at a time.

Add the vanilla extract and white wine vinegar. Incorporate well.

Spoon this meringue mixture into the shape of a large circle onto the baking tray.

Bake in a cool oven for 1-1½ hours.

The meringue Pavlova should be crisp on the outside and soft and marshmallowy in the middle.

Take the meringue out of the oven and place on a large serving plate.

To Assemble and Serve

Spread the whipped cream over the Pavlova. Place the raspberries on the top of the cream evenly. Then place the kiwi slices around the edges.

If you want to be really indulgent, you could add some grated chocolate. The 70% cocoa solids chocolate is the best.

Enjoy!

Lemon and Lime Roulade with a Strawberry Cream Filling

Serves 6

Ingredients
5 Eggs - separated
100g/ 4oz Castor Sugar
Juice of 1 Large Lemon
Grated Zest of 2 Lime
50g/ 2oz Ground Almonds

For the Filling
500g/ 1 lb Scottish Strawberries
Grated Zest of 1 Lime
25g/ 1oz Castor Sugar
285ml / ½ pt Whipped Double Cream
Sieved Icing Sugar for dusting

I like to serve this for a summer Dinner Party

{190}

Method
- Preheat the oven to 180°C/ 350°F/ Gas 4.
- Line a 7 inch swiss roll baking tin with parchment paper.
- Whisk the egg yolks and sugar until pale and creamy.
- Then add the lemon juice and zest of lime.
- Next add the ground almonds and mix well.
- In another bowl, whisk the egg whites until stiff and fold into the lemon and lime mixture.
- Pour into the swiss roll tin evenly and cook for 20-25 minutes.
- When ready, the roulade should be firm and well risen.
- Place the tin on a cooking rack and cover with a clean damp tea towel for 2 to 3 hours.

For the Filling
- Cut the strawberries into thin slices and sprinkle over the lime zest.
- Sprinkle the castor sugar into the whipped cream, followed by the strawberries and mix well.
- Turn the roulade out onto a clean sheet of parchment that has castor sugar sprinkled over the paper.
- Spread the strawberry cream evenly over the roulade.
- Roll it up tightly, removing it from the parchment onto a serving plate.
- Dust with icing sugar.

Chocolate Mousse

Ingredients
225g/ 8oz 70% Plain Chocolate – such as Menier or Lindt
2 Eggs – separated
50g/ 2oz Vanilla Flavoured Castor Sugar
300ml/ 10fl oz Whipped Double Cream
1 tbsp Grand Marnier
Grated Zest of 1 Orange

Method
- First of all melt the chocolate in a bowl over a pan of hot water. Make sure that the bowl does not touch the water.
- When melted, add the Grand Marnier.
- In another bowl whisk together the zest of the orange, egg yolks and sugar. Whisk until it becomes pale and creamy.
- Stir the melted chocolate into the egg mixture and then fold in the whipped cream.
- Whisk the egg whites until stiff and fold in incorporating all the mixture.
- Divide the mousse into 4 glasses and leave in the fridge for a couple of hours to set.

To Serve
- I like to serve some strawberries and orange segments together to go with this mousse, plus some pouring cream of course!
- You can decorate the mousse with half the strawberries or a sprig of mint which also looks good.

Cheese Selection

A selection of cheeses with nice crisp crackers and a fruity Port is a wonderful way to end a dinner occasion.

Scotland's climate and geography are well suited to cheese-making and there are more than two dozen cheese-makers across Scotland. Until relatively recently Scottish creameries primarily produced hard (matured) cheese with Scottish Cheddar accounting for about 75%. However there has been an exciting revival in locally produced farmhouse cheese and an ever increasing range of soft and dolce latté style cheeses available.

My selection of favourite cheeses

Brie de Meaux
Cairnsmore
Cashel Blue
Crowdie
Dunlop
Dunsyre Blue
Lanark Blue
Loch Arthur Farmhouse
Orkney Extra Mature Cheddar

Brie de Meaux

This is the real 'McCoy' of French cheeses. Since the Middle Ages the cheese has captured the hearts of all who have experienced its outstanding taste. It was considered the finest cheese in Europe, thanks to the French Statesman, Tallyrand, who introduced it at a diplomatic dinner. It is produced near Paris, by Societe Fromagerie de la Brie. It is pale yellow in colour, reminiscent of straw. The rind looks like white velvet. The taste is creamy and as the maturing process continues, one detects a subtle, nutty flavour. In 1980, this cheese was accepted into the AOC family.

Country of Origin	France
Milk	Cows' Milk
Texture	Soft

Cairnsmore

This cheese is hard and crusty with red ferments. It is a modern unpasteurised, hard cheese, made from sheeps' milk. The rind developes a series of wonderful mould as it matures. The aroma hits old leather and the texture is firm like cheddar, but more moist. Aromatic and nutty with the sweetness of caramel and burnt toffee, the cheese ripens in 7 – 9 months. It is only made from April to October.

County of Origin	Scotland
Milk	Ewes' Milk
Texture	Hard

Cashel Blue

This cheese is cylinder shaped and made from cows' milk. It has a wet crusty rind with grey moulds. When young, Cashel Blue is firm, yet moist, with a hint of tarragon and white wine. With age, its character emerges, mellowing to a rounder more spicy style. It is available pasteurised, unpasteurised, vegetarian and non-vegetarian. It matures in 8 – 14 weeks and has a fat content of 45%. It is excellent served with a walnut bread. Cashel Blue Cheese is made by Jane and Louis Frubbs.

Country of Origin	Ireland
Milk	Cows' Milk
Texture	Soft

Crowdie (Gruth)

Vegetarian fresh cheese made from skimmed cows' milk. It is usually log shaped but is also sold in tubs. It is said that Crowdie was introduced into Scotland by the Vikings, in the C8th. Called Gruth in Gaelic, it is creamy, yet crumbly with a slightly sour taste. A blend of Crowdie and double cream called Gruth Dhu, has been introduced recently by cheesemaker Susannah Stone. This cheese is formed into oval shapes and covered in toasted pinhead oats and crushed black peppercorns.

Country of origin	Scotland
Milk	Cows' Milk

Dunlop

This cheese was first made ten years ago by Anne Dorward, on her own farm. And today it is produced by Dunlop Dairies. It is a vegetarian, unpasteurised, hard cheese, made from cows' milk. The taste is very mild and buttery, with the sweetness of fresh milk. Aftinage takes 6 months.

Country of origin	Scotland
Milk	Cows' Milk
Texture	Hard

Dunsyre Blue

Cylinder shaped, unpasteurised, vegetarian, blue cheese, made from cows' milk. The moist white rind has a variety of moulds and is wrapped in foil. When aged, the smooth, creamy coloured interior is penetrated by chunky streaks of blue-green mould that imparts a spicy flavour. Dunsyre Blue ripens in 6 – 12 weeks. The producer is Humphrey Errington.

Country of origin	Scotland
Milk	Cows' Milk
Fat Content	45%

Lanark Blue

This Scottish blue cheese is also produced by cheesemaker Humphrey Errington. It has a cylindrical shape and is wrapped in foil. The taste is slightly sweet and the green-blue veins spreading through the cheese are the result of mould having been sprinkled into the milk vat before the cheese curdles. The cheese is then shaped by hand and allowed to mature for 3 months. It is one of the Roquefort style cheeses.

Country of origin	Scotland
Milk	Ewes' Milk
Fat Content	45%

Loch Arthur Farmhouse

A vegetarian, organic, hard cheese made from cows' milk. It usually has a cylindrical shape with a pale brown-grey natural rind. The cheese is firm and quite dry. The flavour suggests a nutty character and has a strong fried onion tang on the finish. It is a traditionally made cloth bound cheddar. Produced by Loch Arthur Creamery and by Camphill Village Trust, the cheese ripens in 6-9 months.

Country of origin	Scotland
Milk	Cows' Milk
Texture	Hard
Fat Content	45%

Orkney Special Mature Cheddar

A block shaped cheese without rind and made from cows' milk. When aged, the cheese contains tiny crystals of calcium lactate. The flavour is nutty and creamy with a hint of burnt onion. The period of maturation takes at least a year. Orkney Extra Mature Cheddar is a great favourite all over Britain and won the Gold Medal at the 'British Cheese Awards 1996'.

Country of Origin	Scotland
Milk	Cows' Milk
Texture	Hard

Game Seasons

Game can only be shot during specific periods of the year. Consequently, it is generally more available during these times and certainly at its best. There is no hunting season for rabbit

Red Deer Stag	1st July to 20th October (Scotland) 1st August to 30th April (rest of UK)
Red Deer Hind	21st October to 15th February (Scotland) 1st November to 31st March (rest of UK)
Roe Buck	1st April to 20th October (Scotland) 1st April to 30th October (rest of UK)
Roe Doe	21st October to 31st March (Scotland) 1st November to 31st March (rest of UK)
Sika Deer Stag **Sika Deer Hind**	1st August to 30th April 21st October to 15th February (Scotland) 1st November to 31st March (rest of UK)
Fallow Buck **Fallow Doe**	1st August to 30th April 21st October to 15th February (Scotland) 1st November to 31st March (rest of UK)
Hare	1st August to 28th February
Grouse **Partridge** **Pheasant**	12th August to 10th December 1st September to 1st February 1st October to 1st February

Scottish Food Producers & Suppliers

Following is a list of suppliers which I frequently use or that have an online shop and mailing service. If calling Scotland from overseas you will need to omit the 0 at the beginning of the telephone number and replace it with your international dialling code plus 44

For many years now I have sourced my meat and game from the award winning butcher, John Anderson, in North Berwick. His meat is outstanding, especially his lamb and beef which is well hung. His awards include The East Lothian Business Association 'Best Retail Business Award 2006' and the East Lothian Slow Food and Drink Competition 'Best Local Supplier in East Lothian 2007'.

'

Clarks Fish shop at Fisherrow Harbour in Musselburgh is fantastic. There is a fresh supply of fish daily, including good quality halibut, scallops and turbot. They also smoke their own salmon, which has a wonderful flavour. It is one of the few places where I can buy quails eggs, which are sourced locally from an East Lothian farm.

MEAT & POULTRY

Andersons Quality Butcher
36 High Street, North Berwick EH39 4HH
Tel: 01620 892964

George Cockburn & Sons
19 Mill Street, Highlands and Islands, Dingwall IV15 9PZ
Tel: 01349 862315

Juniper Green Farmers' Market
Kinleith Arms, 604 Lanark Road, Edinburgh EH14 5EN
Tel: 0131 453 3214

Matheson & Macleod
Lairg Road, Ardgay, Bonnar Bridge IV24 3EA
Tel: 01863 766343

William Mackay & Sons
1 Swanson Street, Thurso, Caithness KW14 8AP
Tel: 01847 892053

The following all sell on-line

Ballencrieff Rare Pedigree Pigs – Pork
Ballencrieff Gardens, Longniddry, East Lothian EH32 0PJ
Tel: 01875 870551
www.ballencrieffrppigs.co.uk

Barkers Highland Beef – Highland Beef
Mid Torrie Farm, Callander, Perthshire FK17 8JL
Tel: 01877 330203
www.scottish-highland-beef-cattle.co.uk

Blackface Meat Company – inc Beef, Lamb, Pork, Poultry, Game Birds, Venison & Goat
Crochmore House, Irongray, Dumfries, DG2 9SF
Tel: 01387 730326
www.blackface.co.uk

Carmichael Estate Farm Meats –
 inc Beef, Lamb & Venison
Westmains Office, Carmichael, Biggar ML12 6PG
Tel: 01899 308336
www.carmichael.co.uk

Damn Delicious – inc Beef, Lamb and Pork
Thankerton Camp Farm, Thankerton, Biggar ML12 6PD
Tel: 01899 308688
www.damndelicious.co.uk

Fletchers Of Auchtermuchty –Venison
Reediehill Deer Farm, Auchtermuchty, Fife KY14 7HS
Tel: 01337 828369
www.seriouslygoodvenison.co.uk

Hugh Grierson – inc Beef, Lamb, Pork & Poultry
Sascha Grierson, Newmiln Farm, Tibbermore, Perth
PH1 1QN
Tel: 01738 730201
www.the-organic-farm.co.uk

Peelham Farm Produce - inc Lamb, Pork & Veal
Peelham, Foulden, Berwickshire TD15 1UG
Tel: 01890 781328
www.peelham.co.uk

Scottish Rose Veal –Veal
Rothesay, Isle of Bute PA20 0QZ
Tel: 01700 503312
www.scottish-roseveal.com

The Store – Aberdeen Angus Beef
Foveran, Newburgh, Ellon, Aberdeenshire AB41 6AY
Tel: 01358 788083
www.thestorecompany.co.uk

FISH & SEAFOOD

Bannerman Co Ltd
Knockbreck Rd, Tain, Ross-Shire IV19 1BW
Tel: 01862 892322
www.bannerman-seafoods.co.uk

Bellhaven Smokehouse
Beltonford, Dunbar, East Lothian EH42 1ST
Tel: 01368 864 025
www.belhavensmokehouse.com

Clark Brothers Fish Merchant
220 New Street, Musselburgh EH21 6DJ
Tel: 0131 665 6181

Inverawe Smokehouses
Inverawe, Taynuilt, Argyll PA35 1HU
Tel: 0844 8475 490
www.smokedsalmon.co.uk

Norman Gallacher
561a Lanark Road, Edinburgh EH14 5DE
Tel: 0131 453 3174

The following all sell on-line

Ardtaraig Fine Foods – inc Salmon & Oysters
Riverslea, Tarholm, Annbank, Ayr, Ayrshire KA6 5HX
Tel: 01292 521000
www.ardtaraigfinefoods.co.uk

Dunkeld Smoked Salmon – Salmon
Brae Street, Dunkeld, Perthshire PH8 0BA
Tel: 01350 727639
www.dunkeldsmokedsalmon.com

Fencebay Fisheries – inc Smoked Salmon, Haddock, Poultry & Meat
Fencebay, Fencefoot Farm, Fairlie, Ayrshire KA29 0EG
Tel: 01475 568 918
www.fencebay.co.uk

Isle of Skye Smokehouse – inc Salmon, Haddock, Kippers & Shellfish
Broadford, Isle of Skye, Scotland IV49 9AP
Tel: 01471 822135
www.skye-seafood.co.uk

Isle of Lewis Smokehouse – Salmon
Mellon Charles, Aultbea, Ross-Shire IV22 2JN
Tel: 01445 731304
www.smokedbyewe.com/

Moray Seafoods – inc Salmon, White Fish, Lobster and other Shellfish
3-15 Low Street, Buckie, Moray AB56 1UX
Tel: 01542 280086
www.morayseafoods.co.uk

Usan Salmon Fisheries - Salmon
The Bothy, Usan, Montrose, Angus DD10 9SG
Tel: 01674 676989
www.usansalmon.com

VEGETABLES, FRUIT & GENERAL PROVISIONS

Mark Murphy & Partners – inc Fruit, Soft Fruit & Vegetables
Newbridge Industrial Estate, Midlothian EH28 8PJ
Tel: 0131 335 3040
www.markmurphyltd.co.uk

House of Bruar – Major on-line retailer of fine food produce
By Blair Atholl, Perthshire PH18 5TW
Tel: 0845 136 0111
www.houseofbruar.com/food-hall-artlfhlhome

Ochil Foods – Major on-line retailer of fine food produce
Hall Farm, Hall Rd, Aberuthven, Perth PH3 1HD
Tel: 01764 662502
www.ochilfoods.co.uk

CHEESES

The following all sell on-line

Caithness Cheese - producer
The Moorings Occumster Lybster Caithness, KW3 6AX
Tel: 01593 721309
www.caithnesscheese.co.uk

Connage Highland Dairy - producer
Milton of Connage Ardersier Inverness IV2 7QU
Tel: 01667 462000
www.connage.co.uk

Island Cheese Company - producer
Home Farm, Brodick, Isle of Arran KA27 8DD
Tel: 01770 302788
www.islandcheese.co.uk

Loch Arthur Creamery - producer
Beeswing, Dumfries DG2 8JQ
Tel: 01387 760296
www.locharthur.org.uk/creamery.htm

I J Mellis Cheesemonger – Cheesemonger
Unit B1A Albion Business Centre 78 Albion Road Edinburgh EH7 5QZ
Tel: 0131 661 9955
www.mellischeese.co.uk

An extensive listing of members of the Scotland of Food & Drink can be found at www.scotlandfoodanddrink.org

Conversions

Liquid

Imperial	Exact Conversion	Recommended ml
¼ pint	142ml	150ml
½ pint	284ml	300ml
1 pint	568ml	600ml
1½ pints	851ml	900ml
1¾ pints	992ml	1 litre

Solid

Imperial	Exact Conversion	Recommended Grams
1oz	28.35gm	25gm
2oz	56.70gm	50gm
4oz	113.4gm	100gm
8oz	226.8gm	225gm
12oz	340.2gm	350gm
14oz	397.0gm	400gm
16oz (1lb)	453.6gm	450gm
2.2lb	1kilogram (kg)	1kg

Oven Temperature Chart

º C	º F	Gas Mark
110	225	¼
130	250	½
140	275	1
150	300	2
170	325	3
180	350	4
190	375	5
200	400	6
220	425	7
230	450	8
240	475	9

Index